BRITISH PARAMOUNTCY AND THE COOCH BEHAR STATE

BRITISH PARAMOUNTCY AND THE COOCH BEHAR STATE

(A STUDY OF THE ANATOMY OF INDIRECT RULE IN COOCH BEHAR)

ANIL KUMAR SARKAR

ABHIJEET PUBLICATIONS

DELHI 110094

ABHIJEET PUBLICATIONS
2/46 Tukhmeerpur Extension
Delhi-110 094
Phone: 011-22960492, 65698474
E-mail: abhijeetpublication@gmail.com

BRITISH PARAMOUNTCY AND THE COOCH BEHAR STATE

First Published 2011

ISBN 978-93-81136-19-5

PRINTED IN INDIA

Published by J.K. Singh for Abhijeet Publications, Delhi-110 094, Lasertypeset by Gaurav Graphics, New Delhi and Printed at Himanshu Printers, Delhi.

Acknowledgements

The present book focuses on the *British Paramountcy and the Cooch Behar State, 1773-1947 (A Study of the Anatomy of Indirect Rule in Cooch Behar)*. This research work is a critical study of the British relations with the Princely State of Cooch Behar during 1773 to last decade of British regime. Instead of concentrating of official British Policy statements alone, this work analyses the underlying patterns and effects of British Indirect Rule on the Cooch Behar rulers and State, and on how the British and Cooch Behar rulers themselves functioned.

By any means, Cooch Behar was a very ancient state and the Cooch Behar Raj was one of the most powerful Kingdoms in this region. Ancient name of Cooch Behar was Kamata Koch Kingdom, which was founded by Viswa Singha and consolidated by Nara Narayan who was the most powerful ruler of this Kingdom. After Nara Narayan, the Rajas of Cooch Behar maintained old traditions and customs in their independent territory with out bothering about changes elsewhere. But the system was broken in the 1773, when the British, in their bid to develop the resources of the Native State for the sustenance of imperial economy, and to integrate this State into a single politico-economic unit, adopted a policy of "Indirect Rule" through the Political Agents.

From 1773 to 1947 was the period of 'Indirect Rule' in Cooch Behar, when for the first time; Political Agents were stationed at Cooch Behar, the State Capital. The Political Agents came with definite instructions to introduce reforms, to develop the resources and thereby to change the State so as to bring someform of uniformity between it and the rest of India.

The work is based primarily on archival sources preserved in the National Archives of India, New Delhi; the West Bengal State Archives, Kolkata; North Bengal State Library, Cooch Behar, District Judge Court, Cooch Behar specially the Secret Reports which the political Agents sent regularly to the Bengal Government. These reports throw light on the 'Annual Administrative Report' of the State. These have, of course, been supplemented by other published documents, Gazetteers, Records, Service-Records, News Papers, Journals, Books and so on.

I have great pleasure in recording my indebtedness to those who helped me in the pursuit of my study. First of all, I wish to record sincere gratitude to my Supervisor, Professor I. Sarkar, Department of History, University of North Bengal, under whose able guidance this work has got the shape in the present form. I am benefited from his scholarly suggestions, academic skills, scientific vision, mentorship patience and encouragement for my study and progress of this work till date.

I also recall Professor Jeraldine Forbes, Department of History, New York State University, Oswego, USA. Who showed her sympathy for this work by rendering few rare books connected with this research work. It was really a rare opportunity for me to develop my idea with a comparative view and knowledge about the work.

I sincerely remember Professor Pranab Kumar Bhattacharjee, formerly Sir Jadu Nath Sarkar Professor of History, University of North Bengal for his valuable criticism and suggestions time and again. I remember the fatherly affection of Dr. Partha Sen, Department of History, Islampur College who encouraged me by his valuable suggestions and relevant books from his own library.

I am also very much indebted to Professor Ratna Roy Sanyal and Professor Ananda Gopal Ghosh, Department of History, University of North Bengal, who helped me whenever required. I am grateful to Prof. Anil Bhuimali, Department of Economics, University of North Bengal, who encouraged me some way or other to finish this research work in time.

In this opportunity may I remember the facilities I received from the Librarian and Staff of the National Archives of India, New Delhi, National Library, Kolkata, West Bengal State Archives, Kolkata, Asiatic Society, Kolkata, North Bengal State Library, Cooch Behar, Record Room, Cooch Behar, A.B.N. Seal College Library, Cooch Behar, North Bengal University Library, University B.T. and Evening College Library, Cooch Behar and so on.

I am also very much indebted to Dr. Nripen Paul and Biswa Nath Das who have ever shown their interest and extended academic help whatever possible for them. I gratefully remember with all humility the counsel, help and encouragement I received from my Colleagues (University B.T.and Evening College and A B N Seal College, Cooch Behar) and friends, like Dr. Chanchal Mondal, Dilip Guin, Amal Ch. Barman, Dr.Bimal Kr. Saha, Anil Biswas, Akhil Sarkar, Tapas Sarkar, Dr. Jaydeep Sarkar, Jitendra Nath Das whose inspirations have done a lot for the progress of this work. My special thanks are due to Smt Dipanwita Das (Sarkar), my wife who always helped me and encouraged to complete the work at the earliest.

Finally, I wish to express my thanks to the typist Dilip Kumar Sarkar of Cooch Behar and afterwards Bubun Kr. Barman who have taken all possible care to type the dissertation and hand over the same in the present form. To the Abhijeet Publications go my earnest thanks for agreeing to publish my book.

Anil Kumar Sarkar

Assistant Professor in History
A.B.N. Seal (Govt.) College
Cooch Behar West Bengal

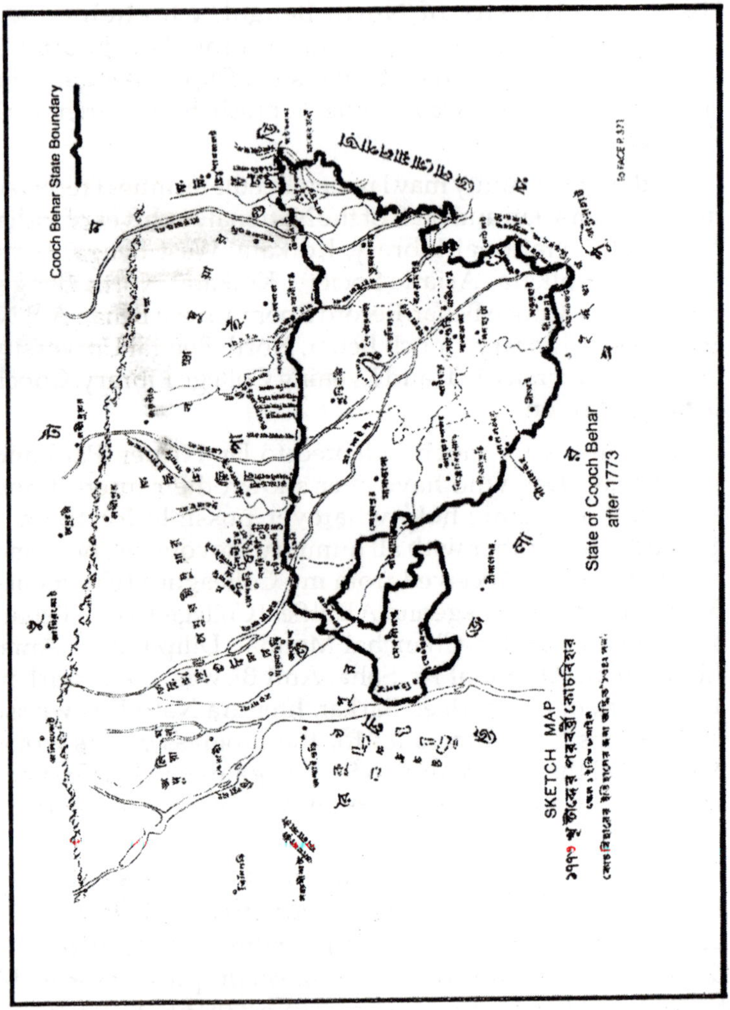
Cooch Behar State Boundary
State of Cooch Behar
after 1773
SKETCH MAP
To FACE P. 371

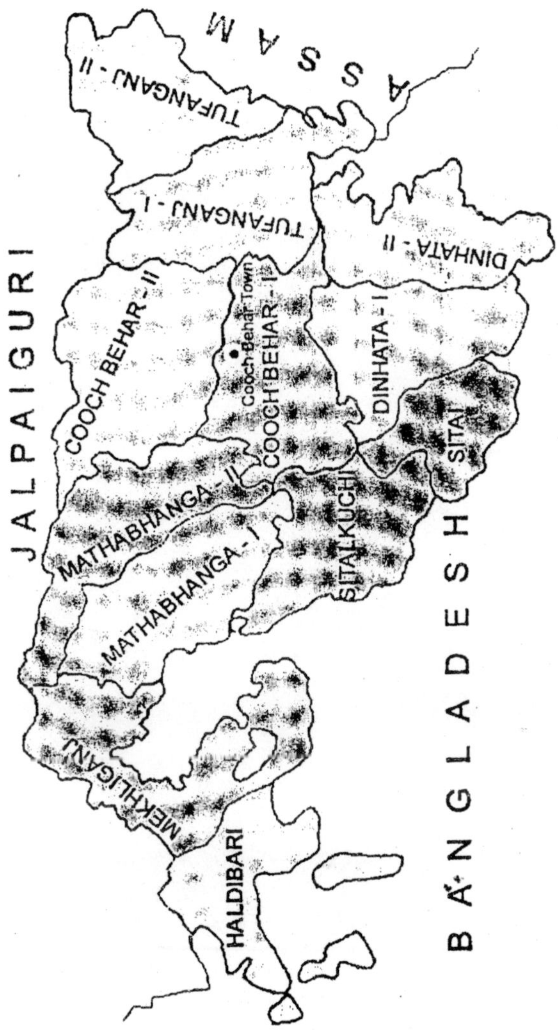

Map - 2. Princely State of Cooch Behar (District of Cooch Behar Today)

Contents

1

Introduction

> "Every real advantage to the people which can be expected from our rule can be secured through a native ruler, with the aid of an English political Agent of average ability, more surely, easily, and cheaply than by any form of direct administration with which I am acquainted"—
>
> Lord Canning
>
> Governor General (1856-1862)

The above was the statement by Lord Canning, Governor General in terms of giving 'real advantage to the people' which could be offered by the British Government and secured 'through a native ruler'.[1]

Many historical empires from Pharaonic Egypt onward have employed indirect rule to extend their influence over disparate peoples with a minimum expenditure in material and human resources. When the British established a vast empire in Asia and Africa, they faced the basic problem because they dominated over the existing political authorities.[2] In most parts of their dominions, they had adopted a system of utilizing the pre-existing political authority, indigenous rulers or traditional chiefs, to carry out most of the processes of local government. This was the situation where an imperial power did not supersede the pre-existing political authority, but established its dominance over it, where traditional rulers were allowed to exercise as before in the local governance. This system is called "Indirect Rule", which stood for a Government through the pre-existing political authority. This was a well established system of British colonial administration and was followed in Africa, Malaya States and elsewhere.[3]

The British system of indirect rule was the exercise of determinative influence and exclusive political control over a nominally sovereign State, a control recognized by both sides.[4] Under it, the administration of native State continued to exist under the aegis of the imperial power. But the traditional rulers, who continued to rule under the domination of the imperial power, had lost their independence and were subject to supervision and owed allegiance to the imperial authority. Under such conditions the district Officers and Residents became the guardians of their power and authority. Not surprisingly, these local authorities came to be identified with the interests of the British. Infact, the British system of indirect rule was motivated by the basic principles of governing a large territory with minimum expenditure.[5]

"Indirect Rule" as an exact term, was not current before the twentieth century, even in India where the practice developed. There, the officials used a variety of labels including "Paramountcy" or "Suzerainty" or "Native Administration" over "princely State", or "Protected Native States" and so on. Much more consistently, however, other imperial administration, following British Indian pattern, commonly used the title "Resident" or "Commissioner" to designate their agent of indirect rule. This continuity suggested that the pattern of indirect rule developed by the British in India served as the model in the later colonial governments.[6] According to Lord Frederick Luggard, father of indirect rule in Nigeria, regretfully conceded in 1922, a reversion to more extensive use of indirect rule was no longer possible in the twentieth century – "It is, of course, now too late to adopt to any large extent the alternative of gradually transforming the greater part of British India into native States governed by their own hereditary dynasties.....and extending to them the principles which have so successfully guided our relations with the native states in Indian itself, and in Malaya in the past".[7]

The present work precisely intends to investigate the British interference in the field of politics, economy and administration of Cooch Behar State from 1773 to 1947. Basically there were two ways to extend British rule: either by conquest and annexation or through inducing the voluntary consent of the Indian people. In the case of princely state of Cooch Behar, British followed the second strategy and course of action. At that time, the British controlled over the state indirectly by inducing their policy and they interfered not only every branches of administration but also controlled the economy and political affairs of the State. Under this stage, Cooch Behar State was dependent on British Government. It is important to note that Viswa Singha, the founder king of the Kamata Koch Kingdom who for the first time assumed the title of Kamateswara and Koch State was also known as Kamata-Behar, especially to the Assamese historical chroniclers. The foundation of the Cooch Behar State under Viswa Singha, in the opinion of Khan Amanatulla Ahmed, took place in 1496.[8] But according to Jaynath Munshi, Viswa Singha is said to have succeeded in 1522.[9] After him, Nara Narayan, his son ascended the throne in the year 1555 A.D.[10] The Kamata-Koch Kingdom reached its zenith under king Nara Narayan who had the credit of incorporating Assam, Bhutan and the whole of North Bengal down to the Ganges up to Gaur. His kingdom was extended as far as Cacher, Sylhet and Manipur in the North East and to the coastal plains of the Bay of Bengal in the south East.[11] After the death of Nara Narayan, the Koch Behar State lost its pre-eminence and gradually declined under the rule of its successive kings. The state became a target of intermittent

Mughal attacks during the reigns of Lakshmi Narayan, Pran Narayan, Mohindra Narayan and Rup Narayan respectively. Koch Behar State gradually tried to establish the relation with Dev Raja of Bhutan. In this situation, force of Bhutanese and Koch armies jointly stood against the Mughals and fought unto the last to push on the Mughal armies on the land of the Koches. The Koch-Bhutanese relations thus opened a new chapter in the history of Cooch Behar. But gradually the Koch-Bhutanese relation did not exist for a long time. Because the Bhutanese army attacked the Cooch Behar State and captured it entirely and there was no single ray of hope in salvaging the seized State in this position. Under these circumstances, there was no way to protect the State without the help of British East India Company. So, Cooch Behar State approached the East India Company for its help to drive out the Bhutanese forces. The Koch Behar was the only Native State of undivided Bengal. Geographically, it was a part of greater Bengal and occupied a place in the North East corner of the province. The present district of Cooch Behar was bounded on the north by the district of Jalpaiguri; on the east by Goalpara; on the south by Rangpur; and on the west by Rangpur and Jalpaiguri. The State lays between 25^0 57′40″ and 26^{0}32′20″ north latitude and between 88^{0}47′40″ and 89^{0}54′35″ east longitude.[12] Before 1773, the Cooch Behar State had maintained their native character properly and consequently it could develop as an independent character of administration and socio-economic and political system. During the last quarter of the eighteenth century and following a few decades of nineteenth century, the East India Company did not follow any specific policy towards the princely States, although there was growing trend towards their liquidation. During this period, the rulers of Cooch Behar had the credit to introduce not only a systematic administration and polity of their own but also could pursue an independent economic policy for the interest of the State and people. There was also a monetary system of their own and it is likely that they could develop a favourable situation. This can be seen in their policies and steps with regard to agriculture, trade and various forms of commercial activities. The development of minting system and independent monetary policy justified the concrete policy of economic development. At this stage (roughly second half of 19th century), a general tendency was to infuse new administrative principles in Cooch Behar and it was largely facilitated due to the advantage of the minority administration under the Regency.[13] Incidentally, the policy at this point of time, the East India Company followed a policy, which was in compliance with the general attitude towards the state of India which may be taken a policy of dependence on the colonial power.[14]

By extending military help to Cooch Behar against Bhutan, Warren Hastings concluded a treaty with Cooch Behar on 5th April, 1773. It was a very important landmark that after the treaty Koch kingdom became the Cooch Behar State in the year 1773. The Anglo-Cooch Behar treaty did not specifically mention the area of British interference in the State. The political instability and internal strife's within the State of Cooch Behar enquired its occasional interference. This interference, gradually and very systematically began to exert upon the State, which reached its climax during the rule of Maharaja Harendra Narayan (1783-1838).[15] In 1802 Lord Wellesley mentioned, "That the terms of the 3rd Article of the Treaty concluded between this Government and the Rajah in the year 1773 would warrant the conclusion, that it was the intention of the contracting parties that the country of Cooch Behar should be ceded in complete sovereignty to the honorable company. It is however, noteworthy to appear that the East India Company did never implement this condition in any circumstances".[16]

From 1858 to 1947, the British developed an indirect rule, which helped to maintain hegemony in India without any risk of annexation and with the least possible expenditure of personnel and economic resources. Key elements included a hierarchy with the British at the apex and the Princes as vassals, a system of honors, most notably the order of the State of India, and the salute table, which established one's rank in the hierarchy. Although the British frequently argued that such honors had particular appealed to Indians, they themselves devoted much attention to their own position in these ranking systems, which affirmed their superior status in India. Although they took up the course of annexation, the British continued to intervene in the internal politics of the princely states for Political or Economic gain, the gradual involvement of the British as an advisory body to look after the details of administration. The education of Prince Heir according to British models was a more subtle means of influencing the future. Official support for intervention varied and reflected evolving British Priorities and the complex interactions within the imperial chain of command.[17]

There was no cohesion or real subdeterioration in any part of the administration from top to bottom. In this respect, H. Beveridge (Deputy Commissioner of Cooch Behar-1864) observed— "The administration of Cooch Behar has not for many years been that of a purely native state, for ever since the treaty with the British Government it has been powerfully acted upon by European ideas. Its proximity too to Rangpur and the fact of all the *Amlah* being natives of Bengal proper assimilated may of its institution to those of British India".[18]

Michael Fisher, the author of *Indirect Rule in India* studied the British Residency system and he has defined indirect rule in India as the exercise of determinative and exclusive political control by one corporate body over a nominally sovereign state, a control recognized by both sides. As the British's realized their new opportunities and needs, they began to transform their network of commercial representatives into a system of political Agents. From the middle of the 19th Century, the Residency system became one of the Central Pillar of the British Empire in India.[19] The political Agents were, of course, nothing new in the British Indian Administration. The British Residents or political Agents were appointed to act as the "Eyes and Ears" of the Government. The case of Cooch Behar is not an exception. Right from the appointment of Henry Douglas as British Resident in 1789, down to the abolition of this post, there were series of administrative changes and the experiments on Cooch Behar were done by East India Company and the British government being the monitors of the whole situation.[20]

But gradually, they got involved in the administrative affairs and in the long run situation was created whereby, the king of Cooch Behar was made puppet in the hands of the British, considering the above situation of Cooch Behar, the proposed dissertation is a humble attempt to explore how an indirect rule was established in Cooch Behar and the State was gradually passing over to the control at first by the Company Government and after words by British Government. The British Government at this juncture appeared not only as policy maker, but also a de facto ruler. On the whole, the proposed dissertation will thus be an attempt to present such a historical development whereby the princely State of Cooch Behar was gradually succumbed to the grip of the British.

NOTES AND REFERENCES

1. Michael H. Fisher, *Indirect Rule in India: Residents and the Residency System 1764–1858*, New Delhi, 1991, p. 70.
2. D.A. Low, *Lion Rampant*, London, 1973, pp. 10-11.
3. J. Zorema, *Indirect Rule in Mizoram 1890–1954*, New Delhi, 2007, p. 1.
4. Michael H. Fisher, *op.cit.*, p. 5.
5. *Ibid.*, pp. 1-2.
6. *Ibid.*, pp. 4-5.
7. Quoted in Frederick D. Luggard, *The Dual Mandate in British Tropical Africa*, Edinburgh, 1926, p. 196.

8. Khan Chaudhury Amanatulla Ahmed, *A History of Cooch Behar* (Bengali version), 1936, p. 402.
9. Jaynath Munshi, *Rajupakhyan* (in Bengali), (ed). Biswa Nath Das, Calcutta, 1985, p. 15.
10. E.A. Gait in his *'Koch Kings of Kamarupa"* fixes 1534 A.D. as the year of Nara Narayan's accession to the throne. He does not accept 1555 AD as the true date, although this is supported by the Cooch Behar chronicles is urged by him that the last mentioned date (1555 AD) may be at the rejected on the testimony of a silver coin was found some years ago at the Garo Hills and published in the *JASB* for 1875, p. 306.
11. H.N. Chaudhury, *The Cooch Behar State and its Land Revenue Settlement*, Cooch Behar State Press, 1903, p. 230.
12. *Imperial Gazetteer of India*, Vol. X, p. 379.
13. *Cooch Behar Select Records*, Vol. 1, p. 132.
14. Michael H. Fisher (ed), *The Politics of the British Annexation of India, 1757-1857*, Oxford, 2005, p. 12.
15. S.C. Ghosal, *The History of Cooch Behar*, Cooch Behar, 1942, p. 342.
16. *Ibid.*, p. 346.
17. Barbara N. Ramusack, *The Indian Princes and their States*, Cambridge, 2005, pp. 130-31.
18. H. N. Chaudhury, *op.cit.*, p. 245.
19. Michael H. Fisher, *op.cit.*, p. 10.
20. Subhendu Majumdar and Biswanath Das (ed), *Princely Cooch Behar: A Documentary Study on Letters (1790-1863)*, Calcutta, 1990, pp. 6-7.

2

The British Policy of Indirect Rule—An Indian Experience

Throughout the British imperial tenure in India, thier administrators described and categorised Indian legal practice, religious beliefs and rituals, social structures and customs and languages and literatures. British officials in India and in the metropole used these data to construct a static, under developed India that legitimated British political dominance. These data and knowledge imbricated with political power. According to C. A. Bayly, the Indians participated significantly in the creation of the British information order, which remained contested and incomplete.[1] Although these intellectual constructions and scholarship have focused on the directly ruled territory and the people of British India, several subsumed the indirectly ruled domains and peoples of princely States. They included gazetteers that were compendia of geographical, historical and statistical data; the great trigonometrical survey that supposedly provided a scientific skeleton for surveys, mapping and a especial conception of India; and decennial censuses issued from 1871.[2] After 1858, Colonial knowledge specifically targeted the Princes and their States.

British East India Company was concluded treaties

depending on the exigencies of war, financial need, personal inclinations of men on the spot, internal politics of the Company, and a States relationship to the Mughal Empire or other indigenous political entities. The relationship between Company and indigenous rulers was helped to understand from few documents like collection of treaties or other legal documents such as *Sanads* and letters.[3]

Although British indirect rule is sometimes called the treaty system, no more than forty Indian States actually signed a treaty with the Company or its successor, the British Crown.[4] The Company extracted vast amounts of capital from each State, either through tribute or subsidy payments by the rulers or else through the manipulation of trade. The Company reduced the size and effectiveness of the armies under the control of the Indian rulers, banning these armies from employment outside of the State and additionally limiting their use by the ruler for internal purposes such as revenue collection. By transferring military power from the armies of the States to 'Subsidiary forces' (paid for by the State but under control of the Company), the Company made many of the rulers powerless to oppose it openly.[5] Through intervention in the internal affairs of the State, in such matters as the succession of rulers, appointment of officials, judicial authority over the rulers subjects and management of Government, the Company eventually established indirect rule over all the Indian States which did not immediately annex. In the case of Awadh and Hyderabad were compelled to sign new treaties upon their accessions to the gaddi. The interpretation of these treaties became arenas of manoeuvre and negotiation among British Political officers, Indian rulers and their Minister and British and Indian lawyers until the demise of the States in 1948.[6]

The British issued large numbers of *Sanads* and Letters to Indian States more than treaties. Sanads were certificate of protection or recognition. The letters from British Government to Indian States formulated the relationship and British wanted to know the situation and condition of the States. The British also undertook mapping and survey expeditions based on post-enlightenment techniques of measurement and visual representation to create scientific, rational and uniform geographic archive.[7]

The British maps came to define visually their indirect rule over Indian States for British and Indian audiences. As Matthew Edney has argued, "boundaries were no longer vague axes of dispute (frontiers) between core areas of Indian politics but were configured as the means whereby those core areas were now defined. Political territories were no longer delineated with respect of the physical features that characterised or bounded them; nor were they defined by the complex feudal interrelationships of their rulers". [8]

The British East India Company sometimes sent their officers to conclude the treaty, and sometimes became diplomatic agents of the Indian States. The Agents always tried to build-up the good relations between the Indian States and British and they became involved in the internal administration of States and extended British control in myriad ways. Maps and surveys, revenue settlement reports, ethnographic reviews and genealogical accounts contributed to the colonial intellectual construction of Indian society in areas of indirect as well as direct rule. Besides being used by the British to conquer and control Indians and to legitimate their own policies and actions, these texts influenced Indian intellectuals, administrators and rulers of Indian States in their constituton of political reality.[9]

Durbars, the formal occasions when the princes met with British representatives either local Political Agents, the Viceroy, or more rarely Members of the Royal family encoded British ideas about their relationship with Indian Princes. As durbars became more frequent with easier transportation by Railway, their protocol became more precise. Regulations evolved about where a prince greeted the British Official upon arrival, how many officials accompanied the British official and the prince, seating arrangements, and appropriate dress. These rituals were most elaborate for the highly coveted status symbol of a visit by a Viceroy or a Member of the British Royal family to an individual princely State. British Government wanted to maintain good relationship to the princely State and they went to the princely State for Pig-Sticking, Polo and Tiger shooting.[10]

Bernard Cohn has argued that after 1858 the British emunciated "two divergent or even contradictory theories of rule: one which sought to maintain India as a feudal order, and the other looking towards changes which would inevitably lead to the destruction of this feudal order ......If India were to be ruled in a feudal mode, then an Indian aristocracy had to be recognized and/or created, which could play the part of 'Loyal feudatories' to their British queen".[11]

During the time of Company regime, the East India Company appointed officers to work after the commercial and the administrative branches and later on revenue collection, judicial work and relations with Indian States came under their supervision. Those who negotiated with Indian States were called foreign or political officers as required. Michael Fisher has outlined the appointment of Political officer of three presidencies "three broad phases in the development of the political service under Company rule. From 1764 to 1797 residents and political Agents were diplomatic agents negotiating between equals. By 1840 there were 116 Political Officers who exercised increasing hegemony vis-à-vis the princes. From 1841 to 1856 their member contracted to fifty one as fewer political Officers were posted to Indian States".[12] In 1843 the Government of India organized a 'Foreign Department' that oversaw relations with frontier areas and external States such as those in the Persian Gulf as well as the princes. In 1914 this entity was renamed as the Foreign and Political Department.

British policies about when and how to intervene in the princely States had long vacillated. In the early 1800s the Court of Directors in London, desiring cheap administration enjoined its Servants 'not to interfere in the internal affairs of other States.' Its officers in India often thought otherwise. In 1825 Charles Metcalfe, then Resident at Delhi and proposing intervention in a disputed succession at Bharatpur claimed "we are continually compelled to deviate from this rule, which is found untenable in practice".[13]

During the 1830s and 1840s the British remained ambivalent. In Rajputana, the British alarmed by the influence of militant Nath ascetics over Maharaja Man Singh II of Jodhpur, actively pursued the expulsion of the Naths.[14] However, they refused to mediate in the more isolated States of Jaisalmer and Bikaner. This oscillation between intervention and laissez – faire continued after 1857. Which they assumed a less overt profile in princely States affairs, the British argued that they retained the right and responsibility to mediate to ensure good government. The occasion for such interference from three clusters: succession, especially when adoption or minor rulers were involved; disputes between princes and their nobility; and rationalization of a State's administration. The British methods of intervention included 'advice' to a ruler, participation in a minority administration, the education of young Princes, and 'suggetions' about the appointment of Minister.[15]

The British government published the *anads* in 1862 and Princes of different States received the *Sanads*, which permitted the adoption of children according to Hindu and Muslims laws. But adoption *sanads* were a double-edged boon. While they assured the preservation of princely dynasties, "they also proclaimed that the British Government would recognise and confirm any adoption of a successor made by himself or by any future chief of her State". [16]

The British Government gradually claimed that no succession, whether or not adoption was involved would be valid without their assent. A State might not lapse, but the British could exert significant influence at the crucial transfer of power from one generation to another. One succession case occurred in Cooch Behar State. When Maharaja Harendra Narayan died, Sibendra Narayan, the eldest son became the king of the State. But his accession to the throne was challenged by his younger brothers, particularly, Brojendra Narayan and Yogendra Narayan; they took the cue from their late father, Harendra Narayan who never wanted his eldest son to become his successor. Macleod, Scott and Jenkins (Commissioners of Cooch Behar State) informed the British Government at different times about the unfavourable attitude of Harendra Narayan towards his eldest Son, Sibendra Narayan. In 1824 British government did not give ear to their allegations and Sibendra Narayan's succession to the throne was recognized by the Government.[17] So, the British Government always wanted to recongnise their favourable person when the question of accession to the throne arose.

The adoption cases occurred in different princely States in Indian context. The adoption case in Baroda, a commission of inquiry was investigating changes of misgovernment and attempted assassination against Gaekwad Malhar Rao, Maharani Jamnabai, the widow of Malhar Rao's predecessor, was 'allowed to adopt..................................(any one) whom the Government of India "may select" as the most suitable person'.[18] The British, desiring to rationalize the administration and the Maharani, wanting to delay any challenge to her authority, both preferred to have a minor adopted. Other adoptions that would set precedents included those at Kolhapur in 1871; Udaipur in 1874 where the Maharani and the State Council selected the heir, the Maharana Sambhu Singh having died without adopting an heir; Aalwar in 1874-1875; Dhar in 1890, and Jhabua in 1893.[19]

According to K.M. Panikkar (Diplomat Historian), the British Governor General (1869 to 1872) Lord Mayo established the practice of forceful intervention during minority administration.[20] The British officials frequently degenerated local appointees to Councils of Regencies as motivated by self-interest.[21] In this situation, Councils gradually rationalized princely administations according to British models that furthered British economic and political interests. They tried to reorganize administrative structures and judiciaries, State managed, forests and most importantly, land revenue settlements. These settlements measured land, defined those who were responsible for land taxes, the major source of State income, the set rates. They always maintained economic and social hierarchies in the princely States where agriculture was even more dominant than in British India.

In western India, the peak year of 1876–1877, almost half of the total princely area was under minority administration.[22] Under minority administration of Baroda (1875-1881), the British Government controlled the economy policy and also the whole administration. In Hyderabad, Mir Mahbub Ali Khan succeeded to the *gaddi* in 1869 at the age of 2 and was only invested with full powers in 1884. Although Salar Jung, the diwan, and Nawab Shams–ul–Umra Amir–I–Kabir, a prominent Noble were to be co-administrators, the Dewan recognized the British right 'to associate themselves with the education of the Nizam and the mode of administration of the State during his minority.'[23] At that time British secured substantial economic concessions during this period. One of the most important things was to have Hyderabad underwrite at ruinous financial terms the construction of a broadgauge railway connecting it with the great Indian peninsula Railway along a route that served British military strategy and not the economic growth of the State.[24]

Minority administrations in Rajputana and the Punjab States and extensive British involvement raised other issues. During the minority of Mongal Singh in Alwar from 1874 to 1877, Alfred Lyall, the Agent of Governor General for Rajputana said, "The natural tendency of a system which makes the political Agent necessarily responsible for good government during a minority is, I think, to draw the whole conduct of affairs more and more within his personal control. This tendency should, if possible, be to a certain degree guarded against, in order that the transfer of power at the end of the minority should not involve a radical change of system." [25] According to Colonel P. W. Powlett, the political agent interpreted this warning as a good reason for developing a State bureaucracy that would continue the British influenced system inaugurated during a minority.

Patiala State had minority administations 1860 to 1910. Ajit Neogy discussed how the British felt that Indian members of the Regency Council during the minority of Mohindra Singh during the 1860 s had ruined the character of the ruler and the quality of the administration.[26] During the minority of Maharaja Bhupinder Singh, the British Government controlled over subsequent Council of Regency and Major F. Popham (Political Agent) revised the land settlement in 1901 and J.O. Warburton (Political Agent) recognized the police department.[27]

Cooch Behar State had minority administration from 1790–1801,1866–1883 and 1923–1935. During the minority of Harendra Narayan from 1790–1801, successive British Residents managed the Cooch Behar State or Commissioners like—Henry Douglas, Andrew Bruce, Towers Smith, Richard Ahmuty and Henry Wagner.[28]

The administration of the State by the British Agents during the minority of Harendra Narayan was on the whole, commendable. Henry Douglas and successive Commissioners pioneered land reformers, streamlined revenue administration and revived the moribund economy of the State.[29] During 1864–1883 and 1923–1935, Regency Council managed the administration. The British Government always wanted to give good administration because they had their own interest to capture the mind of princes and their peoples indirectly. One way was to exploit the advent of minorities in the states to implement reforms directly through British guardian-administrators. As Table 2.1 shows, such opportunities were relatively plentiful.

Table 2.1: Incidents of Minorities in the State of Orissa, 1882-1932

State	*Years under minority administration*	*State*	*Years under minority administration*
Athgarh	14	Khandpura	10
Athwallik	7	Kharsawan	11
Banna	12	Mayurbhanj	16
Baramba	35	Narsingpur	35
Baud	12	Nayagarh	34
Bonai	23	Nilgiri	20
Daspalla	15	Pal-Lahara	30
Dhenkanal	30	Patna	21
Gangpur	4	Ranakhol	10
Hindo	4	Ranpur	0
Kalahandi	32	Saraikela	0
Keonjhar	21	Talcher	11

Source: Ian Copland, *The Princes of India in the Endgame of Empire, 1917-1947*, 1999, p. 19.

Tripura's position among the princely States was a unique one in the sense that it was conquered but not annexed, nor any treaty was concluded between the State and the English authority in India to brace the former in the status of protected ally. On the other hand, the State enjoyed at least technically an 'independent Tipperah' in official parlance in so far as the Hill territory was concerned.[30] The authoritative version of Aitchinson's "a collection of Treaties, Engagements and sanads" underwent many changes in its successive editions, the last edition being in 1929 particularly in connection with the social status of the Tripura ruling family. But the independent status of Hill territory remained practically the same as in the first edition of 1862.[31] The Memoranda on the Indian States published under the authority of the imperial

Government in 1940 recognised the sovereign status of the State in the following words, "The British on assuming change in 1765, took settlement of these zamindaries (styled Roshnabad) leaving the hills independent." [32] This admission in the authoritative version of the Government merely implies the theoretical basis, which the Government could hardly refuse to recognize. But it is the practical status that determines the theoretical one, and not vice versa.

In 1866 the word 'independent' was scapped off without making any reference to the Durbar.[33] And 'Hill' was substituted for it. Thus the State came to be known as Hill Tippera till 1920. Only after an exchange of protest notes over years, the Raj could salvage the ancient name of 'Tripura' as the official title of the State. Yet, the appellation of independent Tipperah appeared in the official correspondences in the reign of Birchandra upto 1882,[34] and also in successive regions. The Robkaries (Royal proclamation) appointing the Yuvaraj bear testimony to it.[35] If independent Tipperah; was practically dropped in official correspondences with the Government it occupied its rightful place in all State papers. Of course, it was no compensation for what was lost in the curb imposed upon the Raj by the appointment of the political Agent to the State in 1871 and conferment of the title 'Maharaja' in the imperial Durbar of 1877.

In 1761 the British appeared on the scene of Tripura. They also made and unmade king like the Mughals, sometimes through they're under hand machanisations and sometimes in their law courts when rival claimants of the royal family would start litigation over the *Gaddi* (Royal cushion – throne). Since the time of Durga Manikya every successive Rajah had been required to pay the *Nazar* or tribute fixed by the Britishers on this succession.

The independent status of Tripura in the Hills, though unrestrained by the absence of treaty obligation and given an added meaning by the momentous decision of 1838, had hardly been immuned from the roughshods of the Britishers. The de-stabilization created by the ruling clique resulted in the appointment of the Assistant political Agent as the State Minister. The subsequent dismissal of the Minister by the Rajah gave the Government a rise to intervene in the state affairs. The *Comilla Durber* was shrewdly organized to wring concessions and to bring the State to a position hardly tenable with the concept of independent status.[36]

During the minority regime, the British Government took the responsibility to educate the princes for their own style. The princes had grown up in British cultural heritage and subjects became a panacea. When regency came to an end the British Government motivated the rulers to continue the reforms and practices, which was started by the British in the minority period. Here the British followed two methods—One was the approval of British tutors for the princes if education with in the State but another method was Princes education depended under the guidence of British Residents and Viceroys.[37]

In 1870s the British decided that princes might be better educated as 'traditional' rulers and partners in the imperial enterprise in the Indian equivalent of a British public school. So many colleges were established all over India to give the western education for the indegenious princes as well as Britishers.

During the eighteen century the relationship between a prince and the British paramountcy was dynamic. They were very much involved about intervention or laissez-faire pervaded its promotion of social reform and efficient administration in the princely States. After 1857, the British officials claimed that the Indians themselves would have to reluctant social reform and the imperialists continued to exhort princes to take action on certain issues. For example, in 1861 the British Government stipulated its jurisdiction in prohibiting the *Sati* vigorously, which was still practiced in Rajputana. If a Prince neglected his duty, the British Government threatened to 'consider the propriety of reducing the number of guns with which the chief of the State saluted; to demonstrate the displeasure of the Queen's Government'.[38] So it was clearly indicated that the British Government always against *Sati* system. After 1857, the British Government interested to give good Government to the princes. John Lawrence, Governor General who energetically proclaimed the gospel of public works and Lord Mayo, his successor, fostered greater State control through modernising institutions. The desired reforms include metalled roads and railways, Public health measures, especially piped water, vaccination campaigns and medical dispensaries; and elementary schools. Although some subsequent Viceroys were more low–key, Lord Curzon, Viceroy from 1899 to 1905, epitomised British intrusion in princely administrative affairs and personal lives.[39] Curzon and many British officials were racist in their desire to have the princes confirmed to British constructions of paternalistic and hard working rulers and in their disdain for prince who challenged the self–image of the British as the only progressive administrators in India.[40] During the period of 1905–1910, when Lord Minto became Viceroy and he announced that the British Government did not interfere in any field of Durbars of princely States. According to British political officers, it was seen that reforms within the States saw it as an unwise constraint.

In the words of S.R. Ashton, "non-interference permitted 'a rapid deterioration of administrative standards in the States' and made them 'wholly unreliable allies' since there no longer had the support of their subjects". [41] But he ignored the fact that popular expectations of Governments changed dramatically from 1910 to 1940s and that in 1947, many State subjects still respected and supported their rulers.

On the whole during the period after 1858, the system of indirect rule achieved the goals set for it by the British Government. In its more stable from and after the Mutiny', the Residency system became a model for much of the rest of the Empire.[42] John Malcolm's prescription for the efficacy of the Residencies (1820) thus proved remarkably acute as a prophesy: "........[a] new and different species of rule is to be tried which is to control clusters of states and communities, and to preserve them in temper and in peace without interfering with their internal administration or arrangements ....[y]ou have the choice between this and an indent upon Hertford college (Haileybury, the company's Civilian training center) and Addiscombe (military seminary) for one thousand writers and five thousand cadets, and Feringy Raj ('foreign', i.e. British rule) all over India .... The consequence of the establishment of our direct authority— that our .... Should last fitly years; but if we can continue to keep up a number of Native states without political powers, but as royal instruments, we shall, I believe, exist in India as long as we maintain our Naval Superiority in Europe".[43]

Thus use of Royal instruments developed over time in India indeed held the Empire together untill the close of World War II. India stood as the foundation for the British Empire, the base upon which British imperialism built elsewhere in Asia and in Africa. Expansion in India occurred during the late eighteenth and early nineteenth Centuries; in contrast South East Asia and East and West Africa came under British control from the late nineteenth century onwards. Ideologically, as well as chronologically and economically, India served as the basis for further British advances.[44] As the proving ground for British use of indirect rule, India was believed by the British to have produced the models that were later consciously adopted elsewhere in the Empire. Further, India served as the training ground for many of the officials— both in London and in the field— who directed or carried out later British expansion, India often proved to be the arena in which they received their first, formative experience with shaping or governing non-European cultures and political system. Colonial administrators often seem to have clung to the memory of their first Indian accomplishments throughout the rest of their careers. India provided the guidelines and precedents, although the process of adaptation to local environments in Africa and south East Asia later shifted some of the terms and forms of imperialism there. Despite this adaptation, both the models and the experience gained in India proved to be vital for virtually all subsequent British expansion and colonial administration.[45]

The European Imperial administrations, indirect rule held a number of apparent benefits. Foremost among them, indirect rule implied reduced cost to the Colonial administration, in terms of both civil and military budgets and manpower. The table compares the number of European officials employed in administration for selected African and Indian examples of direct and indirect rule.

TABLE – 2.1

Ratio of European Officials in terms of local Population direct and indirect Rule, Africa and India

Colony or Local state	*Type of Rule*	*European officials*	*Estimated Population*	*Year*	*Ratio nearest 100*
British Kenya	Direct	164	31000000	1930	1: 18900
French west Africa	Direct	526	14500000	1921	1 : 27600
Belgian Congo	Mixed	316	11000000	1936	1 : 34800
British Nigeria and Cameroon's	Mixed	386	20000000	1930	1 : 51800
India (all)	Mixed	950	253900000	1881	1 : 267300
Awadh	Direct	38	11220000	1872	1 :295300
Princely India	Indirect	107	94000000	1947	1 : 878500
Hyderabad	Indirect	2	10668000	1872	1 : 5333000
Awadh	Indirect	2	11000000	1856	1 : 5500000

Source: Michael H. Fisher, *Indirect Rule in India, Residents and the Residency System 1764–1857*,1991, pp. 8-9.

The British in India introduced two ways of imperial control; direct and inditect. Under the former, British officials brought Indian territory under their immediate administration and in the latter form, the British recognized the sovereignty—variously defined at different times—of numerous indigenous rulers, subject to higher British authority, British political advisors, entitled 'Residents' at the courts of these Rules provided the meanings of indirect rule. As the system of indirect rule evolved from the 1760 onward, Residents tried to induce Indian Rulers an official to conform to British expectations and to implement British policy. Residents both helped formulate British policy and more significantly, endeavoured to enforce it through Indian Rulers. These Residents played a particularly crucial role in the establishment and expansion of British rule over India.

NOTES AND REFERENCES

1. C. A. Bayly, *Indian Society and the Making of the British Empire*, Oxford, 1990, p. 32.
2. Bernard S. Cohn, *The Census, Social Structure and Objectification in South Asia*, Folk 26, 1986, pp. 50-38.
3. Barbara N. Ramusack, *The Indian Princes and their States*, Cambrige, 2005, p. 88.
4. *Ibid*, p. 51.
5. Michael H. Fisher, *The Politics of the British Annexation of India 1757–1857*, Oxford, p. 5.
6. *Ibid.*, pp. 7-8.
7. Matthew H. Edney, *Mapping an Emire: The Geographical Construction of British India, 1765–1843*, Chicago, p. 33.
8. *Loc. cit.*
9. Michael H. Fisher, *op.cit.*, pp. 6-7.
10. L. F. Rushbrook Williams, *The History of the Indian Tour of H.R.H. the Prince of Wales*, 1922, Calcutta, p. 22.
11. Bernard S. Cohn, *'Representing Authority in Victorian India'*, in Eric Hobsbawm and Terence Ranger (eds), *The Invention of Tradition*, Cambrige, 1983 p.166.
12. Michael H. Fisher, *op.cit.*, pp. 54-59.
13. *Minute* by Sir Charles Metcalfe, 1825, in Sever, Documents, Vol. I, p. 145.

14. David N. Lorenzen (ed), *Bhakti Religion in North India; Community Identity and Political Action*, New York, 1995, pp. 120-132.
15. *Ibid*, pp. 106-107.
16. *Coming to Hindu Rulers*, sever, Documents,Vol. I, p. 245.
17. *Cooch Behar Select Records*, Vol. II, p.132.
18. Fatesingh Rao P. Gaekwad, *Sayajirao of Baroda: The Prince and the Man*, Bombay, 1984, p. 41.
19. Ajit Kr. Neogy, *The Paramount Power and the Princely States of India, 1858-1881*, Calcutta, 1979, p. 110.
20. K.M. Panikkar, *Indian States and the Government of India, London*, 1930, p. 56.
21. *Ibid.*, pp. 76-77.
22. Copland, *British Raj*, pp. 138, 300, 316.
23. Vasant Kumar Bawa, *The Nizam between Mughals and British: Hyderabad under Salar Jang –I*, New Delhi, 1986, p. 52.
24. Bharati Ray, *The Genesis of Railway Development in Hyderabad State: A Case Study in Nineteenth Century British Imperialism*, pp. 45-59.
25. Edward S. Haynes, *The British Alteration of the Political System of Alwar State: Lineage Patrimonialism, Indirect Rule and the Rajput Jagir System in an Indian "Princely" State, 1775-1920*, S H 5, n. s. 1989, pp. 27-71.
26. Ajit Kr. Neogy, *op.cit.*, p. 76.
27. Surender Nath Ray, *A History of the Native States of India, Vol. I*, Calcutta, p. 95.
28. Jaynath Munshi, *Rajupakhyan*, pp. 89-99.
29. Harendra Narayan Chaudhury, *The Cooch Behar State and its Land Revenue Settlement*, Cooch Behar, 1903, pp. 320-21.
30. Aitchison, C.U., *A Collection of Treaties, Engagements and Sanads*, Vol. I, Calcutta, 1862, p. 77.
31. *Ibid.*, p. 79.

32. *Memorandum on the Native States,* Delhi, 1940, p. 104.
33. Mackenzie, *A History of the Relations of the Government with the Hill Tribes of the North-Eastern Frontier of Bengal,* Calcutta, 1884, p. 272.
34. *Tripura State Memorandum,* No. 2, Exhibit B, Appendices X, XII and XXIV.
35. Datta, D. C. and Banerjee (ed), *Rajagi Tripura Sarkari Bangla,* Agartala, 1976, pp. 37 and 41.
36. *The Indian Mirror,* Calcutta, dated, 1st July, 1894; The *Englishman,* Calcutta dated 5th February, 1894.
37. Barbara N. Ramusack, *op.cit.* p. 114.
38. *Ibid.,* p. 115.
39. *Ibid.,* p. 117.
40. *Ibid.,* pp. 117-118.
41. Ashton, S. R, *British Policy,* pp.197 –198.
42. Michael H. Fisher, *op. cit.,* p. 458.
43. *Ibid.,* pp. 458-459.
44. Terence Creagh Coen, *The Indian Political Service: A Study in Indirect Rule,* London 1971, p. 125.
45. *Ibid.,* p. 130.

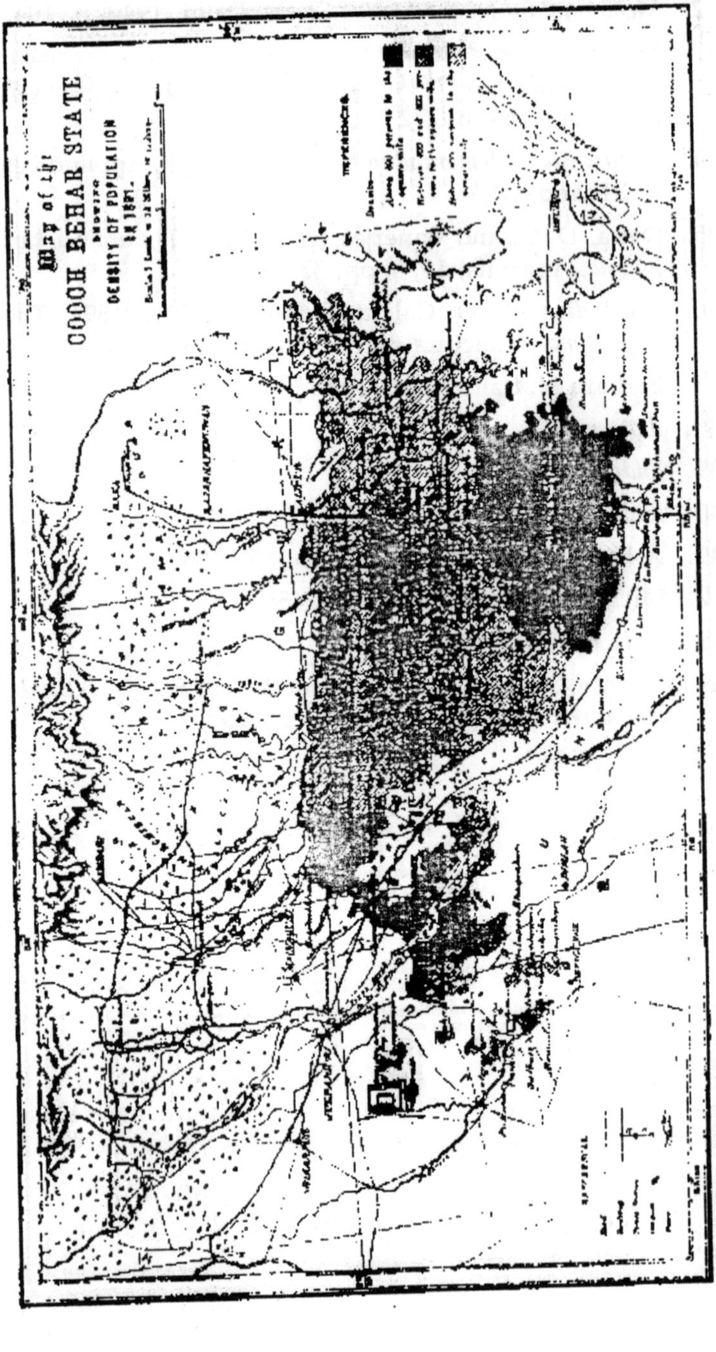
COOCH BEHAR STATE
DENSITY OF POPULATION
IN 1891.

3

The British Construction of Indirect Rule in Cooch Behar

That the British devised and then sustained a system of indirect rule can be experienced from the model of administration they developed in many parts of the World and the case of Kamata Koch Kingdom or Cooch Behar is a glaming example of such a design. Michael Fischer studied the British residency System and he had explained indirect rule in India.[1] When British came to India; their main objective was to develop a congenial position of trade and commerce. But from the second half of the eighteenth Century, they created Political Residency system and gradually the trading interest was shifted to Political strategy and goal. These changes brought with them new relationship between the British and the indigenous rulers. As the Britishers realized their new opportunities and needs they began to transform their network of commercial representatives into a system of political Agents. From the middle of the nineteenth Century, the Residency system became one of the central pillars of the British Empire in India.[2]

The British experimented to maximize their commercial profits, to limit their political liabilities, and to reduce their operational expenses; they first tried to collect revenues through the administration of the Nawab of Bengal. The company soon discovered that this system enriched its servants but did not fulfill their need. So Warren Hastings, Governor of Bengal (1772-73), and the first Governor General of India (1773-85), introduced a more direct system of revenue collection through British Officers, which reached the highest point in the Permanent settlement of 1793. British also created a loyal, dependent intermediary group that would supply fixed revenue.

During the 1730s East India Company signed the treaties with the Indian two small coastal states of Sawantwadi and Jangira and one with the Peshwa regulated maritime and commercial affairs, especially the Suppression of Piracy. The years of 1759-65, the Company did not conclude any formal mechanisms of intervention in internal affairs or restrictions on the external sovereignty of the Indian states. The main purpose of the earliest Treaty was to maintain the friendship and alliance with vague promises of military assistance. In 1765 Robert Clive allied with Shuja–ud–Daula of Oudh to maintain a *Buffer* state between the Company's new base in Bengal and the Marathas. From 1765 to 1772 the administration of Bengal was carried on by two powers—the British and the Nawab of Bengal and hence this system came to be known as the "Dual System" in the history of India. This system of government was introduced by Lord Clive in 1765 and as it proved defective, it was brought to an end by Warren Hastings in 1772. Warren Hastings with great ability and courage faced the hostile powers and thus saved the British dominion at such a critical time.

After the departure of Lord Cornwallis, Sir John Shore was appointed as the Governor General of India in 1793. His time (1793-98) was a period of peace and he avoided any kind of disputes with the Indian Princes. He was a staunch advocate of the policy of non-intervention. He did not interfere in the wars of the native rulers and adopted a policy of strict neutrality. In this way when the Marathas attacked the Nizam in 1795, the latter sought the help of the English on the basis of a former Treaty. Sir John Shore flatly refused to interfere. Consequently the Nizam suffered a crushing defeat at Kharda and was forced to sign a humiliating treaty by which he was deprived of a large portion of his territory. This very fact made a large portion of his territory captured by the Marathas who became very powerful and turned Nizam a dead enemy of the English.

In 1798–1805, the period of Lord Wellesley and his *Subsidiary* Alliances, he inaugurated the second major phase of the evolution of the treaty system. When Lord Wellesley came to India in 1798, the English Company was passing through one of its most critical times, on the other side the English were surrounded by enemies and every-where the French infiuence had greatly increased. After pondering over the whole Problem very thoroughly Lord Wellesley gave up the policy of non–intervention and neutrality followed by Sir John Shore and adored the "Forward Policy" of interfering in the internal affairs of the Indian states. He perfected the subsidiary system and forced all the Indian States to accept it at any cost. Some of the Indian States did not find it suitable to accept and got ready to measure sword with the English. But Wellesley, like a true Statesman, faced all his enemies one by one and won success in the end. Lord Minto, the governor –general from 1807 – 1813, is usually characterized as a pacific interlude between two expansionists. Thomson has described Minto as "Quiet and friendly" and a writer of letters that were "witty and observant, strangely modern in tone".[3] While Minto remained steadfast in not extending Company Protection to the Rajput states, he transplanted several clumps, of smaller chiefs into the soil of British indirect rule.

The arrival of Lord Moira, later on became Lord Hastings, as Governor General in 1813, accelerated the incorporation of the Indian States on to the treaty map of India and inaugurated the era of Subordinate isolation for Indian Princes. Lee Warner portrayed Hastings as lacking Cornwallis faith that Strong Indian States would encompass weaker ones, and become good neighbours, on the model of Ranjit Singh, but also not believing as Lord Dalhousie would, that the good of the people required annexations.[4] Although most commentators mention that Hastings concluded more treaties than any other governor general. He was also a major participant in rounding out the company's directly controlled territories. Administrative rationalization and social reforms were dominant. British concerned after 1823, annexations continued, especially on the borders of the company domains. When Dalhousie appointed Governor General (1848-56), he did not reintroduce a policy of annexation but naturally intensified it.[5] He extended the boundaries of the British Empire in every possible way and made it the only power in India. He introduced the doctrine of lapse greatly added to the territory of the company; it created very baneful influence on India.

After 1857, the British expansion over the Indian State were ended because the Queen Victoria's Proclamation of 1858 which guaranteed the rule of the loyal Princes of India. So the British Policy was changed its course of action. The number of Indian States and their relation with the British were stabilized. The British imperial administrators and officials held up the system of Indirect Rule in India as the model to be follow by much of the rest of the empire. The images of Indian rulers, loyal to the core, and the residents as their paternalistic guides became a matter of faith with in the empire.

The British system of indirect rule over Indian States and a limited ray even in directly ruled areas such as Bihar and the United Provinces provided a model for the efficient use of scarce monetary and personnel resources that could be adapted to imperial acquisitions in Malaya and Africa. Thus there were multiple reasons why the British continued a system of Indirect Rule after they were clearly the dominant power in India.

The origin of the Kamata Koch Behar can be traced back as early as to the Sixteenth Century. There is a great deal of security leading to some academic controversy about the way ancestry of its original founder. The credit of founding the Kamata Koch Behar goes without any shade of doubt to Viswa Singha, popularly known as Bisu. It is said that the Kamata Koch Behar could maintain her character of independence for a long time. But during the reign of Maharaja Dhairyendra Narayan, the independence of the Koch dynasty was under question. The reign of Maharaja Lakshmi Narayan, the supremacy of the Mughals of Koch Behar, was established on the Kamata kingdom, but Maharaja Mod Narayan recovered his independence. British East India Company's intervention in the affairs of Koch Behar presents an interesting narrative. British expansion in North-East Bengal was not so rapid as in other parts of the Country.[6] English East India Company's relations with Cooch Behar in 1772 was the stepping-stone of the British imperial expansion in the Northern Frontiers of Bengal. In the year 1772, Khagendra Narayan, the Nazir Deo[7]of Koch Behar applied to the East India Company for help against Bhutan, who had commenced hostilities and carried away the Raja and Dewan Deo[8] of Koch Behar as Prisoners.

The English East India Company had a soft corner to the State of Cooch Behar because they had a motive and plans to control over the State by any means. For this purpose, Company agreed to offer the military protection of the Cooch Behar State against the enemy of the Bhutiyas. But at the same time, there was no other way to save the throne of Viswa Singh than by seeking the support of the Company. The East India Company's policy in this area as mainly dictated by consideration of trade and commerce with the Himalayan States and the country beyond. It is true that the company's main occupation as traders and also desire to make territorial acquisitions. Firminger wrote " ..... We find that the company was on that whole, averse to the acquisitions of "Territory" or "Possessions" and that their servants in Bengal, when actuated by some momentous emergency were unwilling to interfere in native politics or to depart from the position of Traders". [9] The Court of

Directors had given some direction in their letter dated February 16, 1771, "Remember, we are not fond of much territory, especially if it lies at a great distance from you or is not pretty near the waterside, nor indeed of any, unless you have a moral assurance if it will contribute directly to our real benefit".[10] According to Dr. Surendra Nath Sen, "The growth of British Power in India has perhaps no parallel in History. It was not a case of outright conquest of one country by other but a story of slow penetration in which the people of the land themselves helped the intruders".[11]

Although British indirect rule is sometimes called the treaty system, Company wanted to enter into the Indian Princely States for this system. In case of Cooch Behar, Company also followed the same way. When Bhutanese captured the entire Cooch Behar there was no chance to save the State. At this stage, Nazir Deo Khagendra Narayan in consultation with other dignitaries of the state approached the East India Company for the help to drive out the Bhutanese forces. In the opinion of Joynath Munshi, It was promised to the Company on behalf of the minor king of Cooch Behar that a sum of rupees One Lakh would be paid to it if it could succeed in freeing the state from Bhutanese control. But the offer was not acceptable to the Company which wanted a sum of the annual revenue of the state as price for its help in expelling the Bhutanese and protecting the state in future.[12] However, a treaty was signed with the East India Company in 1773.[13] The Nazir Deo concluded the treaty on behalf of the infant king, Dhairyendra Narayan and the Company force facilitated quick despatches to Cooch Behar. Bhutanese were defeated by the Company's force and Dhairyendra Narayan, the abduct king of Cooch Behar was ultimately released in 1774. W.W. Hunter remarked about this treaty, "that the option and ratification, implied in clause – 9, does not appear to have been carried into effect. It is also noteworthy that the half of the revenue to be paid to the English Government, is clearly marked out as a tribute and not as a tax, by the circumstance that its amount is to be fixed once for all, at a date which is twenty years prior to the permanent settlement of Lord Cornwallis."[14]

5th April, 1773[15] a treaty was concluded and following subjects were mutually agreed on:-

1st – That the said Raja will immediately pay into the hands of the collector of Rangpur Rs.50,000 to defray the expenses of the force sent to assist him.

2nd – That if more than Rs.50,000 are expended, the Raja make it good to the Honourable the English East India Company , but in case any part of it remains unexpended that it be delivered back.

3rd – That the Raja will acknowledge Subjection to the English East India Company upon his Country being cleared off his enemies, and will allow the Cooch Behar country to be annexed to the Province of Bengal.

4th – That the Raja further agrees to make over to the English East India Company half of the annual revenues for Cooch Behar for ever.

5th - That the other mighty shall remain to the Raja and his heirs for ever provided he is firm in his allegiance to the honourable united East India Company.

6th – That in order to ascertain the value of Cooch Behar country, the Raja will deliver a fair last bud of his district into the hand of such person as the honourable the President and Council of Calcutta shall think proper to depute for the purpose, upon which valuation the annual Malguazari, which the Raja is to pay, shall be established.

7th – That the amount of Malgu-zari settled by such person of the Honourable the East India Company shall depute shall be perpetual.

8th – That the Honourable English East India Company shall always assist the Raja with a force when he has occasion for it for the defence of the country, the raja bearing the expense.

9th – That the treaty shall remain in force for the space of two years or till such time as advice may be received from the count of Directors, empowering the president and council of ratify the same for ever.[16]

British first step, after the conclusion of the Treaty was to protect the Cooch Behar State against Bhutia. Firstly, English East India Company defeated the Bhutias and occupied the main fort of Behar. After that, the Bhutias took shelter at *Chechakhata* from where they made proposal for peace. British were compelled to attack Chechakhata because Bhutanese attacked the English troops continuously without any information. Lastly Lt. Dickson who captured Chechakhata and his opinion was, "the Bhutias behaved with amazing bravery, but their daring courage was only productive of a greater slaughter. They often rushed upon our bayonets and met their death at the very muzzle of our pieces. At Cooch Behar I fought for glory. But here I was obliged to fight for life".[17] To the British, the victory against Bhutan was a "costly" one.[18] Ultimately, the Bhutanese foreces lay down their arms and Dhairyendra Narayan, the abducted King of Cooch Behar was ultimately released in 1774.

By the treaty of 1773, Cooch Behar came out, as is a tributary State. It was admitted that the State of Cooch Behar had made only a partial and voluntary surrender of its rights and maintained its independence, unimpaired in its domestic administration.[19] It was pointed out that "he (the King of Cooch Behar) was left in the possession of the two great marks of sovereignty, the right of coining money impressed with his own name, and the administration of justice".[20] But the following events of the State marked by internal feud, discords and dissension opened the floodgate of interference and involvement. By the English with domestic affairs of the state on the hollow pretext of upholding the treaty at the initial stage.

In 1783, after the death of Dhairyendra Narayan, the critical situation arose in Cooch Behar State. The clash between Nazir Deo, Khagendra Narayan and Sarbanand

Gosain led to a coup in June, 1787 in which the latter along with Harendra Narayan, the minor king and his mother, the widow of Dhairyendra Narayan were seized and confined at Balrampur, a place where Nazir Deo had a permanent residence. Harendra Narayan's illegal confinement did not go unnoticed by the English Government. English Government was sent troops immediately for the release of the King.

For this complex situation at Cooch Behar brought home to the Company the need for an enquiry Commission to look into every detail of the native administration and "to make a report on the pretensions of the rival parties, on various subjects connected with the State of the Country, and on the mode in which English influence should be exercised for its better management in the future".[21] A Commissions consisting of Lawrence Mercer and John Lewis Chauvet, was appointed in April, 1788 which submitted its report on 10th November, 1788, the Subject was the nature of the treaty and the situation of the Cooch Behar State. In Cooch Behar treaty, East India Company had not at that time any desire to establish authority or territorial expansion, their main object was gaining money. There was an undefined expression regarding "Subjection" of the King, but it may be that this was written for facility in releasing money. There is no mention in this treaty that any rights or power befitting an independent King like declaring war, Concluding treaty, striking Coins, maintaining an army, internal administration etc. were curtailed or that political connections with other Royal powers were prohibited.[22] We had seen the same strategies were taken by the British Government of Princely States in India.

The Commission had given their opinion about the treaty, "It will be admitted, that under a liberal construction of the apparent object and spirit of the treaty no advantage can justly be taken of the loose and un-defined expressions of "Subjection" and "annexations". That no diminution of the independent right of the rajah within his own government was intended is obvious from his having been left in possession of the two great characteristics of sovereignty, that right of coining money impressed with his own name and the administration of Justice and from this considerations collectively, our construction of the treaty, is that Cooch Behar was thence forward to be regarded in the light of a tributary district, deriving protection from the state to which for that purpose, it made a partial and voluntary surrender of its rights; but maintaining in its domestic administration its independence un –impaired".[23] On 13th May, 1789, Lord Cornwallis passed a resolution to the Report of the Commissioners.[24] The Court of Directors was supported and approved on the 19th May, 1790 A.D.[25] The Commissioners, Mercer and Chauvet had mentioned that the interest of the weaker of the contrasting parties might suffer if the stronger party be placed in the position of a judge.[26]

On the question of minority regime and the misrule by the State officials of the Cooch Behar Lawrence Mercer and John Lewis Chauvet recommended to the British Government to appoint the Resident.[27] The Government accepted the recommendation of the Commissioners and appointed Henry Douglas, British Resident in Cooch Behar in 1789. It is true that the British wanted to form their network to control over the Indian Princely States to enter the political agents or resident. We have seen that the Residency system became one of the central pillars of the British Empire in India.[28] Lord Cornwallis appointed the British Commissioners of the unsettled affairs in the State of Cooch Behar from 1789 to 1800, which was called the Commissioner's Rule. In Cooch Behar, the Commissioners played a vital role to solve the problem and control the administration. 1789 to 1800, Henry Douglas, C.A. Bruce, T.W. Smith and Richard Ahmuty were the Commissioners. W.W. Hunter said about the Commissioner of Henry Douglas "to have supplanted entirely the authority of the Rani, and her Minister Sarbanand Gosain. He conducted himself all the office, whether judicial or Revenue of the

State or at least Superintendent proceedings of the courts and control their decisions".[29] Henry Douglas wrote "since that time it was suffered a very considerable administration owing principally to the mal administration of the Rajah's Minister, who has not only himself been guilty of the greatest oppressions, but also connived at them in his dependence. Large portions of land have been alienated, a variety of new taxes introduced, every species of abuse committed in the collection of the revenue and the administration of Justice had been perverted to the purposes of emolument. Thus harassed and oppressed numbers of the ryots were obliged to leave their native country and the revenues falling short in consequence of this, and from the alienation of lands, the remaining inhabitants were obliged to make good the deficiency".[30] Douglas solved the different problems and also created some reforms about the State of Cooch Behar. At that time Harendra Narayan attained maturity in 1799 but management of the state was handed over to him in 1801.

Lord Hastings was of the opinion that Cooch Behar was "A tributary State under the protection of the British Government, and depended even for its existence on that protection. He noted the charges against Harendra Narayan and held that the Treaty of 1773 imposes upon the Rajah, the duties and allegiance obligatory and can demand the penalty of a violation or disregard of those duties".[31]

That penalty was not merely the dissolution of the existing alliance but the actual annexation of Cooch Behar to the dominions of the Company. The Governor General, however, did not act at that moment contemplate the measures of assuming the full exercise of its right, but the circumstances in Cooch Behar made it necessary to interfere.[32]

The British policy of the little State of Cooch Behar changed radically as soon as when Wellesley came to power. The Governor General in Council, taking into his consideration the arrangements, necessary to be adopted for future management of that part of the possessions of the Raja of Cooch Behar which were situated beyond the limits of the province of Bengal. On that principal, when the Governor General in Council thought it essential to appoint a commissioner to restore order and tranquility in the unsettled and convulsed State of the Country in the year 1789, and to provide for the management of the affairs of the Rajah. During the minority of the present Rajah, it was expressly declared that it was not the intention of the Government in any respect, to injure the independent right of the Rajah.

It was further declared that, as soon as the Rajah should be capable of taking charge of his State, he would be restored to the full management thereof, and to all the independent rights and privileges, which had been secured to his family by the treaty of 1773.

The Commissioner was, at the same time instructed to transact the business in the name of the Rajah, and to fix his seal to all official papers, and like wise to preside in person on the part of the Rajah in the Courts of Justice.

Under the above circumstances whatever right it had been originally intended was that the Company should enjoy from the terms of the article, respecting the cession of Cooch Behar. The Governor General in Council did not think it would be consistent with the justice and the honour of this Government to assert a title, at this distance of time, to the exercise of any power in that territory, except such as may appeared to be compatible with the construction, which had hither to been put on the treaty, with the measures, which had been in consequence, adopted by the Government relative to Cooch Behar, and with the sentiments expressed on the public records on the subject of that State.

On adverting, however to the tribute, which the Rajah was bound by the 4th article of the above mentioned Treaty to pay to the honourable company to the relation in which the native of Cooch Behar had so long stood towards this Government, with respect to the administration of Justice, and to the wishes, expressed by the Rajah himself in a letter, addressed to the Governor General in Council, on the 9th June 1798, the Government should be pleased to establish such permanent regulations for Cooch Behar as they might think proper, His Excellency in council considers it to be the particular duty of this Government to adopt, with the concurrence of the Rajah, such measures as may be best calculated to enable the Rajah to provide for the regular payment of his tribute to the Company, by the establishment of proper rules for the collection of the Public Revenue, and to ensure a prompt and pure administration of Justice by means of the company's servants, and by extending the principles which have been adopted for that purpose in the company's territories, to Cooch Behar.

In admitting the receipt construction of the treaty as the basis on which the negotiation with the Rajah, for the adoption for further arrangements should be conducted, the Governor General in Council observes that this Government will not be precluded from exercising its right to decide on such points, as have before called forth the interposition and authority of this Government. Of this nature, are the claims of the Nazir Deo and Dewan Deo, upon which, owing to the intricate nature of the claims and the difficulties attending the investigation, on decision had yet been passed.

But neither in asserting the right, or in extending with the Rajah's concurrence the rules, in force in this province for the collection of Public Revenue and the Administration of Justice, will it be necessary or proper to subject the Rajah himself to the jurisdiction of the Courts, which may be empowered to take cognizance of civil and criminal causes in Cooch Behar.

It like wise appeared to the Governor General in Council that, as Criminal accusations had been from time immemorial tried in Cooch Behar by the Hindu Law, it would be advisable that all tribes and mis-demeanours should be tried by that Law, with which modifications and alterations, as may be deemed advisable.

On the ground above stated, His Excellency in Council resolved that a Commissioner be deputed to Cooch Behar to form the necessary arrangement in Concern with the Rajah, for the collection of Revenue and for the administration of justice, and for the adoption of a proper and efficient system of police in the territory of Cooch Behar, and that the Governor General be requested to furnish the Commissioner with a letter, addressed to the Rajah, pointing out the principles, on which it was proposed that the negotiation between this Government and the Rajah should be conducted, and the advantages which may naturally be expected from the adoption for the salutary regulations, which it was the wish of Government to extend to that State.

His Excellency in Council, not being awared of any advantage, which would arise from committing to the commissioner the charge of the collection of the parganas of Bodah and Patgong, or the other Mahals which had been recently annexed to Rungpore, and it being advisable that the undivided attention of the Commissioner should be directed to the formation of the proposed arrangements.

When Harendra Narayan came to Power in 1801, he strongly opposed the British interference with the sovereign authority of the Rajah. British East India Company was withdrawn the Ahmuty, the British Commissioner in Cooch Behar State and to give the whole authority to Rajah Harendra Narayan. After that the British Government made a fresh attempt to get involved in the internal administration of Cooch Behar in some matters. The British Government accepted "the Rajah of Cooch Behar........ as independent Princes, subject only to the payment of the tribute and deemed the consistent with the dignity and how of the British Government to extend the regulations to Cooch Behar, in opposition to the inclinations of the Rajah. And the same time; the Governor General in council........impressed with a strong sense of the expediency of adopting that measure, as soon as may be practicable, with the two consequences of the Raja, with a view to the important benefits which must arise from the establishment of fixed laws and regulations in the territory of Cooch Behar, and from the administration of more laws and regulations by the servants of the Company".[33] John French was appointed to act as Commissioner of Cooch Behar and his first object to establish with the concurrence of the Raja, the Rule of law in Cooch Behar, John French failed to realize the policy towards Cooch Behar and appeared to have interfered with the administration of Justice. But Harendra Narayan was not ready to accept the policy of British Govt. So, British Govt. abolished the separate office of a Resident Commissioner in Cooch Behar and the collector of Rungpore was made responsible for the execution of British policy in the native state. During the period 1805-1813, three successive collectors of Rungpore, Archibald Montgomery, James Morgan, and John Digby were ex-officio Commissioners of Cooch Behar State. In 1813 the British Government found when a serious criminal charge was made against Cooch Behar Raj and John Digby was sent to the Cooch Behar to make investigation. In same year, Macleod Resident Commissioner levelled serious charges against Harendra Narayan but Harendra Narayan proved base-less and "the Government took the Commissioner to task for allowing himself to be carried away by false reports and rumours".[34] The Government wanted to change the policy and so liberal policy was introduced towards Cooch Behar.

The British Government felt the need to appoint a new Commissioner in the changed circumstances following the liberalization of British policy towards Cooch Behar. In 1822, Scott was appointed Agent to the Governor General; the North East Frontier and Cooch Behar affairs came under the Jurisdiction of his office.

The reign of Harendra Narayan was marked by a protected diplomatic battle and clash of interest between the authority of the king and the paramount power of the British. "During this period, the policy of the supreme government towards the country was finally decided upon and its formation was greatly influenced by the attitude of the ruler of the Raj. It was in the reign that the question whether Cooch Behar should gradually pass into a Zamindari of Bengal arose more than one and it was greatly due to the representation of the Maharaja Harendra Narayan that it is still a feudatory State......".[35]

It had been noted before that Harendra Narayan was the last ruler of Cooch Behar to oppose the British policy. After Harendra Narayan, no ruler of Cooch Behar State stood against the British Government or British policy. Sivendra Narayan, was also the secret choice of the British as the future ruler of Cooch Behar.[36] So, It was very interesting that there was no need to follow any strong policy towards Cooch Behar and also no question of annexation. After the death of Harendra Narayan, the eldest Son Sivendra Narayan became the king of the State. But his accession of the throne was challenged by his younger brother. Harendra Narayan did not want his eldest son to become his successor. Macleod, Scott and Jenkins informed to the British Government about the unfavourable attitude. Lastly British Government decided to give recognition to Sibendra Narayan's succession to the throne as a King of Cooch Behar State. During the reign of Sibendra Narayan the economic condition of the state was developed. Sibendra Narayan paid all the taxes due at the time of Harendra Narayan. W.W. Hunter said, "By rigid economy and with the indulgence of Government, he cleared off all the arrears of tribute which encumbered the state. He also free himself entirely from the private debts inherited from his father, and is said to have by considerable accumulations. He paid particular attention to revenue matters and to the improvement of his estates at Rangpur; and was as careful in the regulation of his own expenses as in the supervision of the public offices of finance".[37]

Sibendra Narayan played an important role to introduce the western education in Cooch Behar State. Sibendra Narayan was assured of every co-operation by the British Government in the establishment of a school at Cooch Behar. One thing is rightly pointed out that Sibendra Narayan accepted the British over lordship. In 1841 Sibendra Narayan married to two girls and for this occasion Lord Auckland Governor General of India presented him with a pair of gun, 23rd August, 1847. Sibendra Narayan died at the age of forty-nine. After the death of Sibendra Narayan, his heir son became the king of Cooch Behar, but at that time he was minority King and he went to take education from Krishna Nagar.

After Sepoy Mutiny, the British Govt. was forced to pursue soft policy towards the native States. The policy of "Doctrine of Lapse" was withdrawn. In 1862, the Government of India delivered the *Sunnad* to Narendra Narayan, the King of Cooch Behar, on the Condition of their remaining loyal to the Crown and faithful to their engagements with British Government. In 1848, Secretary F.J. Halide wrote a letter to Secretary J.P. Grant (Bengal Govt.) "His Honor in council concurs in the opinion of the Deputy Governor that it is desirable that the territory of Cooch Behar, so long as it may managed or superintended in its management, should be placed under the jurisdiction of the Government of Bengal, all questions, however. of an important Political bearing an important Political bearing being referred for the orders of the Supreme Government".[38] British Government introduced some reforms in the administration of the State. Under guidance of British Commissioner, the character of the administration began to change. "The feudal character of the administration gradually changed into constitutional character".[39] An education, Narendra Narayan was very interested to spread the English education all over the State. So Harendra Narayan Chaudhuri (author of History of Cooch Behar) said "presented a purse to Colonel Jenkins, worthy Colonel, however, advised the Maharaja to found an English School was established in 1861, which was named Jenkins School".[40]

After the death of Maharaja Narendra Narayan in 1863, his minor Son Nripendra Narayan was the next ruler of the Cooch Behar State, on 15th January 1864. British Government recognized Nripendra Narayan as a king –

"It is expedient to recognize Nripendra Narayan, the only legitimate Son of the Late Maharaja, expressed distinctly before his death, where in possession of his senses, Nripendra Narayan is accordingly recognized and confirmed as Raja of Cooch Behar, in succession to his father, the question of investing him with the title of the "Moharaja" remaining in abeyance until he arrives at his majority".[41]

For this situation, Agent, North East Frontier, Major William Agnew wrote a letter to Maharani of Cooch Behar State—"I am instructed to acquaint you that the appointment of a British Commissioner to manage the Estate, during the minority of Nripendra Narayan, is considered by the Government to be imperatively called for, as the only means of effectively providing for the care and education of the young Rajah, for the security of the Government Revenue and for the defence of the Bhooteah Frontier, for which the Government is responsible".[42] The Maharani of Cooch Behar was agreed about the opinion of British Agent and British Government sent Colonel Haughton to Cooch Behar State "to take charge of the entire administration in all its branches, exercising the subject to the control of the Government through the Agent, North East Frontier, the full authority of the Rajah, except in regard to the grant of land, pensions or gratuities, and the confirmation of capital sentences, but exercising it, for the present through the existing administrative machinery, and making no material change in the present arrangements without the sanction of the Government. An important part of his duty to will be to see that the young Rajah is properly cared for and brought up, and the Rajah's education with hereafter became a subject of paramount importance".[43] The British Government ordered to Colonel Haughton "you shall exercise your authority subject to the direct control of the Government, and that, so far as regards the internal administration of the Cooch Behar state, the Agent, North East Frontier shall be relieved of all responsibility. You will therefore, correspond direct with the Government on all matters connected with your charge".[44]

When he succeeded the throne, he was one year old. During his minority the charge of the administration was placed in the hands of a Commissioner appointed by the Governor. From his reign the administration of Cooch Behar entired the modern phase. The Commissioner of Cooch Behar was vested by the Government with full authority of the ruler of the State.

From 1864 to 1883, the Cooch Behar State was ruled directly by the British Commissioners. The Maharaja Nripendra Narayan attained Majority and was formally installed on 8th November, 1883.The charge of the administration was formally made over to him by the Lieutenant Governor of Bengal and at the same time, Commissioner's post was withdrawn.

In 1883, Maharaja Nripendra Narayan became majority and lieutenant Governor of Bengal; Sir Reverse Tomson gave recognition as king of Cooch Behar State. Tomson wrote" I am present here today to formally transfer to your personal rule of this State of Cooch Behar, which owing to your long minority, has been now for 20 years under the British Control. I speak no conventional terms of gratification, when I say that it is exceedingly great pleasure to me to preside by virtue of my office at this ceremony, because in the first place I have had the pleasure of knowing you now for several years and have the confidence (which I don't think is misplaced) that in delegating authority to you we are delegating that which is not only yours by rightful inheritance, but by the fair equipment of your mental and bodily powers to exercise the prerogative of a high position; and secondly because in discharging finally the trust which the government has assumed and has exercised these many years, it does so with the justifiable consciousness of a duty which has been successfully and honourably fulfilled. I have the less hesitation in saying this because personally I can claim nothing of the praise which is due to those who have laboured incessantly for your interests in the advancement of the state; but I should be wanting in my duty if I failed to take advantage of this the first public opportunity which I have had of testifying to the merits of an administration, which in the hands of my friend, Lord Ulick Browne, the present Commissioner of the Rajshaye Division, has achieved results in the well ordered organization of a state which has now to be transferred to your own management".[45]

Nripendra Narayan gave answer–"I desire publicly to express my grateful recognition of the many obligations by which I myself individually and my state are bound to the British Government, and to assure you of my unfaltering loyalty to her Gracious Majesty's Government at the hands of whose representatives I have ever received such consideration and under whose fostering care my country so materially prospered".[46]

On 9th November, 1883 British Government formed 'Raj Sabha', Commissioner Major Evence Gordon prepared a memorandum for ruling the State. Maharaja did not change anything. Memorandum is like that – "The Maharaja is satisfied that the present system of Administration, under which the State and its people have prospered and made such satisfactory progress, and for which he is much indebted to the British Government, leaves nothing to be desired, and that if he were in a position to assume the functions and duties of supervision now discharged by the Commissioner and in some cases by the Government, no change whatever would be necessary". [47] The Cooch Behar State Council on Rajsabha had resolved to act for the present in some important matters by and with the advice of a council. It was a general sketch of the system that all matters depended may have the approval of the British Government in regard to it. The Cooch Behar State Council was consisted of three members with the Maharaja as President. The members were the Superintendent of the State, the Dewan and the experienced Judicial Officer whose services the Maharaja hoped to obtain from the British Government. In the absence the Superintendent would act as the Vice President of the Council. It is interestingly that the Superintendent was an agent of the British Government.

Three members were entirely independent of each other. The Superitendent of the State supervised direct and control the administration of criminal justice and the Police, Military, Jail, Public Works, Education and Audit departments and he would be Session Judge, hearling all criminal appeals which ordinarily lies to session judges, but would not act as a civil judge, except when sitting in council. Appointment of all officers and the all pensions granted and all engagements made and all laws passed by the British Government on our behalf were hereby confirmed.[48] According to Rivers Tomson (Lieutenant Governor of Bengal), Maharaja developed the good work, which had been begun, and to make the independent management of his State by native agency a model of administration.

Maharaja Jagaddipendra Narayan became the King of Cooch Behar State in 1922. Maharaja was the last ruler of CoochBehar State. The Government of India had recognized the succession to the *Gaddi* of Cooch Behar of his Highness Maharaja Jagaddipendra Narayan Bhup Bahadur. He always welcomed the British policy. In his time, there was no confrontation between Maharaja and Paramount power.

NOTES AND REFERENCES

1. Michael H. Fisher, *Indirect Rule in India Residents and the Residency System 1764-1858*, p. 6.
2. *Ibid.*, p. 41.
3. Edward Thompson, *The Making of Indian Princes*, p. 150.
4. Lee Warner, *Native States*, pp. 102-03.
5. Lee Warner, *The Life of the Marquis of Dalhousie K.T.* 2 Vols, Ireland, 1904, p. 46.
6. S.N. Sen, *Pashcim Banglar Patra Samkalan (1859)*, Introduction.
7. Nazir Deo was an Important Post of Cooch Behar State Administration. He was the Commander of the army.
8. Dewan Deo was an Important Post of Cooch Behar State administration. He was in charge of Civil affairs in the State.

9. W.K. Firminger, *Introduction to the Fifth Report*, Introduction, p. III.
10. *Ibid.*, p. 16.
11. S.N. Sen, *op.cit.*, p. X.
12. Jaynath Munshi, *Rajupakhyan* (in Bengali), (ed), by Biswanath Das, pp. 56-57.
13. Khan Chaudhury Amanatulla Ahmed, *A History of Cooch Behar* (Bengali), p. 378.
14. Hunter, W.W., *A Statistical Account of Bengal*, Vol. X, p. 419.
15. S. Turner, *Embassy to Tribal*, p. 373.
16. *Cooch Behar Select Records*, Vol. 1, pp. 245-246.
17. For Section Cons. March, 1773, pp. 1-2.
18. Arabinda Deb, *Relations between India and Bhutan*, p. 76.
19. W.W. Hunter, *op.cit.*, p. 416.
20. *Ibid.*, p. 419.
21. *Ibid.*, pp. 417-418.
22. S.C. Ghoshal (ed), *A History of Cooch Behar*, p. 394.
23. Mercer and Chauvet's Report, (CBSR), Vol. II, p. 189.
24. *Ibid.*, p. 202.
25. Resolution by the Government on Cooch Behar Report, 13th May, 1789, Mercer and Chauvet's Report, (CBSR), Vol. II, p. 202.
26. S.C. Ghoshal, *op.cit.*, p. 396.
27. Extract from the Proceedings of the Governor General in Council under date the 7th August, 1813, Cooch Behar Select Records, Vol- I, pp.225-231.
28. Michael H. Fisher, *op.cit.*, p. 41.
29. W.W. Hunter, *op.cit.*, p. 420.
30. Douglas wrote the letter to Governor General of Corn Wallis (Letter No. I).
31. Letter to Mr. John French from G. Dowdes –Well Sec. X to Government, 18th Feb, 1805.
32. Harendra N. Chaudhury, *The Cooch Behar State and Its Land Revenue Settlement*, p. 257.

33. *Ibid.*, p. 257.
34. *Cooch Behar Select Records*, Vol. II, pp. 45-46.
35. *Ibid.*, p. 424.
36. Biswanath Das and Subhendu Majumdar, *Princely Cooch Behar: A Documentary Study on Letters (1790-1863)*, p. 42.
37. Durgadas Majumdar, *West Bengal Disrict Gazetteer*, Koch Behar, 1977, p. 39.
38. Ratna Roy Sanyal, *The Raj and the Princely State of Cooch Behar, A Study of Anglo–Cooch Behar Relations 1772–1839*, p. 168.
38. H.N. Chaudhury, *op. cit.*, p. 317.
40. *Ibid*, p. 284.
41. The Administrative Reforms Introduced by the Commissioners found in Chapter X and XI.
42. *Cooch Behar Select Record*, Vol. II, p. 189.
43. *Ibid.*, p. 254.
44. *Ibid.*, p. 256.
45. *Annual Administrative Report of Cooch Behar State*, 1888-1889, p. 12.
46. *Loc.cit.*
47. *Koch Behar Gazetteer, 1884*, pp. 44-46.
48. *Ibid.*, pp. 49-52.

Maharaja Nripendra Narayan
(architect of Modern Cooch Behar State)

Colonel Houghton (Agent of North East India and Commissioner of Cooch Behar State)

4

Imperialism in the Making

4.1 Appointment of the Political Agents

In the second half of the 19th century, the Indian sub-continent was finally divided into two distinct identities; the British Indian States, and the princely India. Initially, there were two ways to extend British rule: either by making conquest over the Native States or through inducing the voluntary consent of the Indians. The British Indian States, they ruled directly but the princely States, they ruled indirectly. The Political Agents were, of course, nothing new in the British Indian administration. The British Residents and political Agents were appointed to the more important position to act as the "eyes and ears" of the Government.[1] They were expected, being on the spot, to observe and report regularly on all major events occurring in the states and to recommend appropriate measures where necessary. It was true that the company was, after all, more interested in profit making than in any civilizing mission.[2] During the period of 1870's that the political Agents, as instruments of reform and moderisation was realised, though such possibilities were anticipated by Lord Canning as early as in 1860.[3]

It was to be noted before that the Kamata Koch kingdom or Koch Behar State became Cooch Behar State during the period of Anglo-Koch treaty of 1773. After that, the situation became complicated, when there was the clash between Nazir Deo Khagendra Narayan and Sarbananda Gosain (a mentor and favourite of the Queen). At that time Harendra Narayan, the minor king and his mother were sized and confined at Balarampur.[4]

For this stage, the East India Company sent an enquiry Commission to see into every detail of the administration. The enquiry Commission gave report to the Government and the Government accepted the recommendation of the commissioners and appointed British Resident or commissioner in Cooch Behar State in 1789.

During the period from 1789 to 1800, Henry Douglas, C. A. Bruce, T. W. Smith and Richard Ahmuty were efficient Commissioners of Cooch Behar State and they played a vital role in controlling the Cooch Behar's administration. Their main objective was to take care of the land revenue administration. Lord Cornwallis assured the Raja of Cooch Behar (the Minor king Harendra Narayan) that the appointment of commissioner was temporary, and not permanent.[5] A huge number of letters were exchanged with the Governor General, the Secretary and Sub-Secretary to Government and the Commissioners of the Cooch Behar State from time to time.[6] The Commissioners informed to the Government of their day to day decisions with regard to the numbers of problem of the State. Infact, the Commissioners became the real administrator of the State. During this period, stepes were taken up for the betterment of the Revenue administration.[7] Other issues relating to administration or functioning of the State affairs, however remained untouched. Henry Douglas was appointed the first British Resident in Cooch Behar in 1789 with a monthly salary of Rs. 1,500.[8] He was instructed to manage the administration of the State and was also to guide the king properly and make him fit for administration. Incidentally, When Douglas took over the charge as British Resident or Commissioner in Cooch Behar, Harendra Narayan was only ten years old. The British Government was taken carefully so far as the young Raja's education and all the responsibility in this respect were concerned.[9] Jay Nath Munshi was appointed as one of the tutors of Harendra Narayan.

It may be noted that some remarkable changes were brought in by Henry Douglas in the administration of Cooch Behar. Some of them were really outstanding and these are as under- (a) The Commissioner's signature and seal must be put-on side by side with that of the Maharaja.[10] (b) Separate criminal and revenue courts were established and respective seal for each court was introduced. Henry Douglas' first attention was to look into the revenue administration of Cooch Behar State. When Douglas took charge of his office, the condition of the exchequer was very deplorable. He informed the detailed report to the Governor General on the condition of the State. He observed, "From the monthly accounts, which have been transmitted to your Lordship will have been perceived the very impoverished state of the Cooch Behar Treasury: that the expenses have exceeded the revenue and the deficiency has been obliged to be supplied by loans". [11]

Henry Douglas observed many abuses and irregularities with regard to land Revenue settlement. First of all, there was too many taxes in the State, there was no practice to fix rent.[12] The State was not given the regular deed of agreement to the cultivators. The *Ryot* had to pay ***Nazzars*** and ***Salamis*** to the officials, but there were not clear accounts. Sarbananda Gosain aquared large portion of the lands and Maharani enjoyed the whole of the Raja's private land. For this situation, real revenue of the State gradually deterioted. Besides, the interest on money as reported by Douglas, "has never been regulated except by the avarice of the lender and the necessities of the borrower so that in common 72 percent has been considered as very moderate interest and what almost exceed belief that in many instances which come to my immediate knowledge, 360 present has been exacted. Money landing was so profitable that the Sepoys of the company had to a share in this business. In 1783, Captain Duncanson had lent an amount of rupees

14,901 to the minor king of Cooch Behar. He was not satisfied with an annual return of rupee 21,000 as the interest was considered to be very low".[13] Again he states, "as a result of extortion by the revenue collectors and the exploitation by the money lender a good number of Ryots fled from the state resulting in further reduction of the revenue of the state. Douglas had introduced certain reforms which helped to increase the revenue of the state and provided "great relief to the Ryots too. The first ever settlement was completed under his direct supervision".[14]

Therefore, Douglas had main attention to introduce a uniform system of Revenue collection pattern in the Cooch Behar state. First of all he introduced the *Ijaradari* system in land revenue settlement of Cooch Behar State. Before coming of Douglas, the revenue of the State collected by the State officer was named as *Sazwals*. The land revenue settlement was made annually by the supervision of British Resident of Douglas. Douglas had placed so much faith as a suitable settlement for Cooch Behar.[15]

Charles Andrew Bruce became the Commissioner of Cooch Behar in place of Henry Douglas in 1791. The British East India Company ordered C. A. Bruce to see all the documents with regard to the revenue settlement of Cooch Behar State. Government also gave suggestions to Bruce that he might follow the previous settlement or to prepare any alternative plan which could be different from the system suggested by the previous Commissioner of Cooch Behar State.[16] Bruce gave the proposal to the Government that previous revenue settlement was not sound and needed modifications. There was a serious defect and so he did not want the system to continue. The defect was the villagers and others who let them again the intermediate agents. Bruce gave some proposals to remedy the evils. He introduced his reforms in Boda, Patgram and Purbabhag. For these areas he introduced the farming system. Every village had prepared a farm and the farm was controlled by the ***Pradhan*** or the head Ryots of the village. The Ryots should pay the expense of the village ***Patwaries*** and other charges. Commissioner gave appointment to the pradhan for one year and paid the revenue in installments calculated on their crops. According to Bruce, this system was benefited both the Ryots and British Government. So Government accepted the proposals of Bruce.

After Bruce, W.T. Smith became the commissioner of Cooch Behar State on October, 1795. Smith followed the recommendations of his predecessor Bruce.[17] The British Government wanted to settle the lands problem by granting Pattas to Ryots. It is true that the British Government had a sense of superiority in the field of administration and it wanted to prove its worth in making experiments in the revenue settlement. Cooch Behar was by all means, a State to introduce such a formula from colonial point of view.

After W. T. Smith, Ahmuty became Commissioner of Cooch Behar State in 1797. During his period, the land revenue of the State increased. Ahmuty followed the new system and wanted to ensure a stable economic condition of the State.[18] He observed that the Ryots had no right to till the land permanently and this effected the gross income of the State as well as of the Company.[19] In the given situation, Ahmuty encouraged Ryots to expand more cultivable lands and gave incentive to bring more and more lands under cultivation. He got huge response from the cultivators. At that time there was no system of measurement of lands. Ahmuty at first tried to measure the Ryots' holdings lands and gave *Pattas*.[20] According to Ahmuty, the annual settlement of revenue was not continuing well, so, he raised the term at least five years. It was the first time in History of Cooch Behar State when there was a valid register of the lands.[21] During this period, the Government wanted to set up uniform pattern of revenue collection system in Cooch Behar State, and this principle was first reflected in their revenue settlement and collection. It can be noted here that from 1789 to 1800 Henry Douglas, C. D. Bruce, W. T. Smith, Richard Ahmuty, were successively posted in Cooch Behar, as Commissioners and neither any change nor any remarkable development could be seen in the administrative structure or system of Cooch Behar other than in the Revenue administration.

During the minority period of Harendra Narayan, the British officers controlled the administration of Cooch Behar State. The successive commissioners developed the revenue administration and revived the moribund economics of the State.[22] The British Government withdrew the commissioner in 1801 and the State was handed over to Harendra Narayan. Raja of Cooch Behar State had appointed Kashinath Lahiri as Dewan of the state. Kashinath Lahiri praised the British administration and justice and their (British Officers) contributions to the development of the State.[23]

When Lord Wellesley came to power, the British policy towards the Indian state changed radically. Lord Wellesley was basically haunted by an imperial design and his policy to Cooch Behar is a glaming example of his ambitious plan on the excuse of improving the administration of the State. At that time the conflict was going on between the Raja and the Dewan of the State and on this question the peace of the State was hampered. In this situation, Lord Wellesley communicated his desire to Harendra Narayan to appoint a Commissioner to act in consultation with the Maharaja for the collection of public revenue, administration of justice and of the Police.[24] In January 1803, Lord Wellesley appointed Francis Pierard as a Commissioner for the Cooch Behar State. Harendra Narayan was reluctant to accept the arrangement because according to Rajah of Cooch Behar, it was the interference with the sovereign authority of the Raja. The British Government accepted "the Rajah of Cooch Behar .... as independent princes, subject only to the payment of the tribute" and deemed it inconsistent with "the dignity and however of the British Government to extend the regulations to Cooch Behar, in opposition to the inclinations of the Rajah".[25] British Government wanted to establish with the concurrence of the Rajah for the important benefits, which must arise from the establishment of fixed laws and regulations in the territory of Cooch Behar State. After failure of the Pierard Mission, the British

Government was appointed John French to act as a Commissioner of Cooch Behar in early 1805. John French's primary objective was to establish with the concurrence of the Rajah, the Rule of law in Cooch Behar. At that time Lord Cornwallis became Governor General for the second time. Cornwallis followed the policy of non-intervention to the Native States. On the other hand, Harendra Narayan strictly followed his position. John French was failed in his efforts to convince the Rajah and was not able to deal with Cooch Behar administration. The British Government abolished the separate Commissioner's office in Cooch Behar State. After that, the Collector of Rangpur was made responsible to see the British Policy in the Native State of Cooch Behar.

During the period 1805–1813, three successive Collectors of Rangpur – Archibald Montgomery, James Morgan and John Digby were the ex-office commissioners of Cooch Behar State.[26] They maintained the relations with Cooch Behar State from Rangpur. In this time, Nazir Deo or Dewan Deo made serious criminal charge against Cooch Behar Raj. Dewan gave the report to the British Government that huge number of corruption, anarchy oppression and bloodshed were going on in the state. The British Government sent John Digby to the Cooch Behar State to make investigation. He was treated with disrespect and hostility, the British Government became furious "to adopt immediate measures for restraining his (Harendra Narayan) vicious and depraved conduct, and asserting the right of the British Government to interfere in the internal administration of the affairs of Cooch Behar....................for the prevention of anarchy, oppression and bloodshed".[27] We have said before that the relations between Rajah of Cooch Behar and Dewan were not so good. During this time, Harish Chakraborty, a *Pujari* or worshipper of idols was in the service of Dewan Deo. Maharaja of Cooch Behar became angry and Harish Chakraborty was imprisoned and later he died. Dewan Deo gave allegation that Harendra Narayan caused the death of Harish Chakraborty.[28] The Collector of Rangpur interfered enormously in the matter of Cooch Behar administration. The Commissioner gave more important position to Dewan than the Raja. On 7th August, 1813, a Government resolution was passed to follow the betterment of Cooch Behar administration. But their actual objective was to interfere the administration justice, the settlement and the collection of the revenue.[29]

After that Lord Cornwallis revived the post of Resident or Commissioner in 1813 and Narman Macleod was appointed as Commissioner in Cooch Behar State on monthly salary of Rs. 1500. Macleod's first target was to establish a raport between the British Government and Harendra Narayan. J. Adam, secretary to the Government wrote a letter to Harendra Narayan that "The just attention and difference with which you have listened to the advice and representations of the Commissioner offered in the name and express authority, of the Government, the methods, which you have made, to continue to abide by it, combine to assure me that you are convinced of the sincerity with which the British Government has sought your welfare, and of your determination invariably to act is a manner to merit its confidence and friendship." [30] Mutual trust and cooperation between Raja and British Government did not last long, Macleod interfered all the matters of administration time to time. For this reason, Raja of Cooch Behar was unwilling to help Macleod. The result, Mac leod could not be able to establish peace and piosperity. On the other hand, serious charges revealed against Harendra Narayan that Harendra Narayan met Raja of Nepal and they hatched conspiracy against British Government. But ultimately it was proved baseless and "the Government took the Commissioner to task for allowing himself to be carried away by false reports and rumours".[31]

After this, there was a change in the British policy towards Cooch Behar and it was confined, "to abstain from all interference except in the form of advice and representation in the unlimited management of the affairs of Cooch Behar, and to restrict the powers of the commissioner to the exercise of diplomatic functions only".[32] It is significant here to note that J. Adam, ordered to Commissioner – "It is proper to observe that the less frequently advice is interposed, the more efficacious, generally speaking it is likely to prove, and that it is therefore desirable to avoid as much as possible all interference in point of details, and matters of subordinate importance, which might be likely to produce irritation and disgust, and to reserve the full right and influence which the British representative must possess for occasions of moment. By adhering to these principles and by the observance of a mediate and conciliatory tone towards the Raja, it may be hoped that you will be able to establish an influence over his mind which will eventually effect a considerable amelioration of the system of his government and become productive of reciprocal benefit to himself and his subjects".[33]

The British Government wanted to change the policy and try to follow the liberal policy towards Cooch Beahr. After Mac leod, Devid Scott took charge as a Commissioner of Cooch Behar State in 1822 and he was appointed as an Agent to the Governor General, the North-East Frontier. So, Cooch Behar affairs came under jurisdiction of his office. The Commissioner post was abolished. Devid Scott became the successor of British Agent. He was diplomatically dealing with the state of Cooch Behar. T.C. Robertson became the Agent in place of Devid Scott in 1830. The Agent of North East Frontier did not interfere in the internal affairs of Cooch Behar State.

In 1834 Captain F. Jenkins became the British Agent in North East Frontier and Cooch Behar State was also under his jurisdiction. Captain F. Jenkins visited as the Commissioner to the Cooch Behar State in 1836, 1841, 1847 and 1849 successivly. F. Jenkins was a liberal British Agent and he had seen all the matters in Cooch Behar State sympathetically. First of all Jenkins appreciated Sibendra Narayan's efforts towards the reorganization of the State economy. Jenkins remarked that the State witnessed the "great increase of Population and extension (sic) of cultivation during his reign." [34] The British Government could not fail to take note of Jenkins's assessment and the Court of Directors came to the conclusion that there could not be any considerable "miss-Government" at Cooch Behar.[35] Sibendra Narayan cleared all the arrears of tribute, which encumbered the state. First of all he gave attention to revenue matters and to the improvement of his state. Sibendra Narayan did not confine his attention only to the revenue matters but he also established 'Rajsabha' in 1840, the highest Court of the state. He introduced western education in Cooch Behar. Sibendra Narayan's personal interest in the prohibition of *Sati* did evoke a favourable response from the British Government which in a letter to Jenkins admitted, "...........................it is gratifying to the Government to find the Rajah so well disposed to conform in this respect to the benevolent intentions of the British Government for the general abolition of this is human rite" [36] The prohibition of *Sati* come into effect so late as in 1849 after the death of Sibendra Narayan.

Sibendra Narayan's health condition gradually deterioted and it also affected the internal condition of the state. This situation led to the increasing influence of the bureaucracy in the state affairs. This had even drawn the attentions of Jenkins and he reported to the Government that - "The Rajah, I am sorry to say, is very inattentive to business, partly owing to sick ness, and has entrusted all the affairs of his Raja to two or three Bengalees, who, I fear, commit much injustice" [37] Superintendent of Darjeeling, Campbell charged the Native Government of Cooch Behar of inefficiency and mismanagement contining and he sent letter to Jenkins why he reserved about his role.

Campbell addressed to Government of Bengal to interfere in Cooch Behar matters about the bureaucratic norms.[38] Bhandaree Aye (claim her, step mothers of Sibendra Narayan and a widow of Harendra Narayan) wrote letter to the Governor General that the inefficiency of Brojendra Narayan, corruption of public servants, anarchy, internal feud and total law-less-ness were continued in the state.

She also wrote to Campbell her doubt about the efficiency and neutrality of Jenkins.[39] Government of Bengal wrote to Governor General about the gross maladministration in Cooch Behar State. Incidentally the report of Government of Bengal presented the matter in the style that "............... the management of Cooch Behar during the Rajah's minority, the failure of the Agent to visit that little citation last season, and the insufficiency of that officer's reports, in consequence of that failure, and for the failure of the chief officers of that state to visit him, leaves the Deputy Governor unable to form a satisfactory opinion. His Honour has seen with much pain the evidence, which the papers before him seen to afford of gross maladministration in Cooch Behar............The Government can not but look with society to the receipt of the Agent's report, after he shall have made his long Projected visit to Cooch Behar, and His Honour would recommend that the visit should be made without further delay. The Government will look to him for an unbiased account of the real condition of the country, and for mature advice in respect to its future administration during the Rajah's minority".[40]

Government of Bengal ordered to Jenkins to prepare a genuine statement about the condition of the princely State of Cooch Behar. Because Government of Bengal gave top priority about the opinion of Jenkins. Jenkins visited the Cooch Behar State in February, 1849 and he found that the complaint against mal-administration of the State as false and baseless. Government of Bengal accepted the Jenkin's report on the condition of Cooch Behar State. He observed with satisfaction about the improvement of agriculture and growth of population and that the Ryots had no allegation against the authority. Jenkins mentioned the lapses in to the administration on of the state and the excesses were committed by the Regent, Brojendra Narayan. When he submitted his report to the Bengal Government and he recommended the appointment of British Resident who would advise the Regent in his capacity as a Commissioner. The result the native administration of Cooch Behar controlled properly. But the Bengal Government did not accept any substance in his suggession.[41] The Government of Bengal highlighted all the demerits related with Cooch Behar affairs was responsible the Governor General on the North East Frontier to the Government of India Government of Bengal wanted to take over the administration of Cooch Behar during the minority of Narendra Narayan. For this situation, Cooch Behar came under dual responsibility. Bengal Government suggested to Government of India some possible matters which should be relieved that (i) ordinary administration of Cooch Behar state (ii) Agent of the Governor General, North East Frontier should undertake Government of Bengal temporarily.[42] Government of India accepted the suggestion of Government of Bengal and Jenkins, Agent of the Governor General of India came under Government of Bengal was satisfied with the role performed by Jenkins. Jenkins observed all the matters about Cooch Behar was concerned. According to Jenkins "the general administration, though marked by occasional abuses, appears, on the whole, a fair specimen of native rule, and the great increase of cultivation and the increase of the Ryots, ...are indicative of progress and wellbeing".[43] British Government not only observed the general administration of Cooch Behar State but was also interested to give western education for Cooch Behar Raja. In general view the Agent of Cooch Behar wanted to spread English education all over the State.

In 1860, Jenkins made his tour to Cooch Behar State. He was fully satisfied at the administrative and economic development of the State.[44] In 1861, Jenkins retired from his service but he was Agent of Governor General of North East Frontier for a long time.

After Major Jenkins, Hopkinson became the British Agent of Cooch Behar matters in 1861. Raja of Cooch Behar always trusted to the British Government and Cooch Behar State could not involve itself in sepoy mutiny. The British Government was forced to pursue a soft policy towards the native states after the mutiny. The 'Doctrine of Lapse' policy was withdrawn.

The British Government gave recognition to Nripendra Narayan as next king of Cooch Behar State in January, 1864.[45] Colonel J.C. Haughton, Governor General's Agent, North East Frontier took charge of the state from Hopkinson during the minority of Nripendra Narayan, as commissioner of the Cooch Behar state in February, 1864. The British Government took responsibility in providing care and education of the young Maharaja, for the security of the tribute and for the defence of the Bhutan frontier.[46] The Commissioner of Cooch Behar State had full authority of the entire administration in all its branches, except, in regards to certain specified points, such as the grant of lands, pensions and gratuities and the confirmation of capital sentences. It is also said that no change in present arrangements would be made without the sanction of the Government.[47] Colonel Haughton was continued in his duty still 1873. During this time, British Government also appointed one Deputy Commissioner in Cooch Behar to follow all the matters properly. H. Beveridge was the first deputy Commissioner in Cooch Behar State. One thing is that Colonel Haughton was not only an able man of administration but also could judge the matters on the State properly.

According to Dalton (Deputy Commissioner of Cooch Behar State) "Colonel Haughton appeared to have always exercised the full powers than confided to him and to have done so with a judgment and ability, which combined with the personal interest. Which he displayed is all, even the most trivial matters connected with the administration, fully justified the confidence reposed is him and ingurated that system of judicial and political reform and financial development, which is the hands of his successors have made Cooch Behar what it is." [48] Colonel Brance took charge in absence of Colonel Haughton in June, 1865 untill his return on December, 1866. In 1873, when Colonel Haughton left the Cooch Behar, Richardson and Metcalfe became as

Commissioners upto March, 1874. Then W. J. Herschel was appointed Commissioner and continued his post till 1875. When F.R. Cockerell became Commissioner for one year and Cockerell was the first Commissioner of the Rajshahi and Cooch Behar Division. Lord H. Browne succeeded as Commissioner in 1876 and continued to be at the head of the Cooch Behar administration till the Maharaja attained his majority on October, 1883.

H. Beveridge, the first Deputy Commissioner of Cooch Behar, who took charge on the 4th November, 1864,was succeeded by T. Smith on the 1st May, 1866 and made over charge to Captain W. Lance in 1868. Captain Lance was relieved by W.O.A. Beckett on the 22 December, 1870, whose term was succeeded by Smith, who returned to Cooch Behar in February 1872 and remained to 11th April 1875, when Captain Lewis went on 6 months leave in April 1876 and Mr. JGBT Dalton was appointed to officiate and subsequently confirmed in the post. When he went on privilege leave, Captain Evans Gardon officiated till his return on December, 1882.

The British Government tried to form administrative arrangements when Nripendra Narayan became the Maharaja of the State. The Commissioner of the Rajshahi and Cooch Behar Division framed a memorandum of administration and it was adopted by His Highness. A Council of State was established in 1883 with His Highness as President, and three members namely – the Superintendent of the State, the Dewan and a judicial Officer. It is said that in absence of President on the day "the Superintendent will act as vice President of the Council".[49] The Superintendent supervised directly and controlled all the departments. He was appointed justice of the peace with-in the State for the trial of European British subjects intriguing the laws of the country.[50]

From 1883 to 1913, Lieutenant Colonel A. Evans Gordon, E.E. Lowis, D.R. Lyall, Major J.R.C. Colvin, E.L.L. Hammond, A.W. Dentith, B. Ghose were appointed Superintendents of the State and Vice President of the State Council

Incidentally none of them had brought about any significant change of the administration of the State rather were ornamentals to look after the affairs of the State as a whole.

The term of Mr. Dentith's appointment as Superintendent of the State and Vice President of State Council, having expired on the 22nd April, 1913, His Highness was pleased to appoint E.W. Collin, ICS to the post with the approval of His Excellency the Governor of Bangal in Council.[52] The Government of Bengal in their order No. 646 PD; dt 2nd May, 1912, vested the Commissioner of the Rajshyee division with the powers of a political Agent for the State of Cooch Behar for the purpose of the provisions of the Indian Extradition Act., 1903 (XV of 1903).[53] The Government of India in their letter No. 5300 P, dt. 8th November 1912 were pleased to order that Magistrates or Officers exercising magisterial powers in Native States shall be regarded as Magistrates for the purposes of Rule 4 of the Rules under the Indian Security Act, 1886.[54]

The post of the Superintendent of the State was abolished under His Highness orders on 1st June, 1916. His Office since then was styled Office of the General Department of the State and the Vice President of the State Council was placed in charge of controlling over all the Departments.

Millingan (1920-1923), Major Charles Terench (1923-1926), Colonel Hutchinson (1926-1931), Major K.A.G.E.Gordon (1931-1934), Colonel J.A.Bret (1934-1936), J.D. Taison (1936) were incharge but they had only supervised the departments under their jurisdiction.

His Highness the Maharaja Bhup Bahadur was invested with full ruling powers on the 6th April 1936 by His Excellency the Right Hon'ble Sir John Anderson, Governor of Bengal, who came to Cooch Behar for the purpose.[55] L.G. Wallis was appointed Vice President of State Council up to the 21st November, 1939. Government of India maintained the Residency system till 1947. Change of new format partially His Highness the Maharaja Bhup Bahadur, as President consisted of Rai K.C. Ganguli Bahadur, Acting

Vice President and Revenue Member. The Chief Minister was appointed to be the Ex-Officio Vice President of the State Council.

In the meanwhile, however, there was a change in the format of the State Council of Cooch Behar. The State Council was named as State legislative Council in 1940 in which His Highness the Maharaja Bhup Bahadur was designated as President. The post of the Vice President was given to the Revenue member who virtually got the portfolio of the Cheif Ministership of the State.

4.2 Paramountcy and Judiciary — Conflict and Assimilation

After conclusion of the Anglo Cooch Behar treaty, 1773, there was no berrier to interfere all the affairs, both internal and external. At that time the State administration was in chaotic condition for the maintenance of the army and to ensure stabilizing of the State. Because the clash between Nazir Deo Khagendra Narayan and Sarbanand Gosain (sided wih the Queen) reached at the zenith. In this situation, British power got involved into the State administration of Cooch Behar. The British East India Company appointed Commissioners to see the entire administration. The Governor General in Council assured the temporary management of Cooch Behar with a view to protect it from the ignorant and designing persons. The State was managed and controlled by successive British Residents or Commissioners during the minority of Harendra Narayan (1789–1800 AD).

As noted earlier during 1789–1800 AD, the British Commissioners like Henry Douglas, C.A. Bruce, T.W. Smith and Richard Ahmuty were posted in Cooch Behar but no remarkable improvement was visible in any sphere other than that of Revenue administration. They tried to improve the Revenue administration.[56] The British Commissioners were not very much interested to solve the maladies in other matters of the State or Society. There was no remarkable change in the administration of Justice.[57] In 1801, the Commissioners' regime in Cooch Behar State was withdrawn and the State was handed over to Harendra Narayan. Anglo– Cooch Behar relation was in complicated phase when Harendra Narayan came to power and took the administration of Cooch Behar in his own hand. Cooch Behar State came under the supervision of Rangpore's Commissioner. In this situation Lord Wellesley, the Governor General, decided that the Commissioner would not interfere in the administrative affairs of Cooch Behar but would give advice to the Raja.[58]

Harendra Narayan had passed his boyhood under the care and guidance of British Commissioners and at that time anti British attitude grew up because he was always ill advised by his evil Councilors to whom the Commissioner's regime was a great hindrance to the fulfillment of their own interests. Lord Wellesley wanted to improve the administration of the State and he communicated his desire to appoint a Commissioner for Cooch Behar to act in consent with the Maharaja for the collection of public Revenue, administration of Justice and of the Police.[59] According to Lord Wellesley "The Raja of Cooch Behar have not only been permitted subsequently to the date of the treaty, to coin money, to administer Justice, and to exercise other power of sovereignty, by that their rights to exercise of such powers has been fully and unreservedly acknowledged by the British Government of India".[60] The British Government appointed Commissioner constantly to introduce British Regulations in Cooch Behar but strong opposition to such measures came from the part of Maharaja Harendra Narayan.

Wellesley assured to Maharaja Harendra Narayan that in introducing the new arrangement the British Government had no intention to subject the Ruler of Cooch Behar to the jurisdiction of a British Government. British Government had firm determination to introduce the general Regulations in force in the province of Bengal to Cooch Behar.[61] Harendra Narayan felt that the transfer of the administration of Civil and Criminal justice into the hands of the Company was against the honour and independence of his Raj. [62] So, Maharaja was always against the appointment of Commissioner for Cooch Behar State. In these circumstances, British Government had to follow the policy of "wait and see" with regards to the introduction of British Regulations into Cooch Behar. The Cooch Behar State faced anarchy, oppression, bloodshed and corruption and British Government wanted to prevent all these things and protect the State. Maharaja Harendra Narayan firstly dismissed all the corrupted officials immediately and Macleod (British Commissioner) helped properly. For these reasons, Harendra Narayan changed his attitude against British Government and he was pleased. So Maharaja asked for the Government's assistance for a better system in the administration of justice, which totally collapsed in Cooch Behar. The British Government prepared a thorough scheme of reforms for implementation in the judicial administration of Cooch Behar.[63] Harendra Narayan requested the British Government to preserve his work and dignity.[64] British Government accepted His request. Harendra Narayan agreed to the British proposal of reforms in the administration of justice in Cooch Behar. As a result, the conflict between Maharaja Harendra Narayan and British Government in the question of judicial reforms came to an end.

After Harendra Narayan, Sibendra Narayan became the Maharaja of the State of Cooch Behar and British Government gave him recognition. In His reign Cooch Behar State became financially better than the reign of Harendra Narayan. Sibendra Narayan's one important achievement was judicial reforms. He established 'Rajsabha', the highest Court of the Cooch Behar State in 1840. Dewan Kali Chandra Lahiri and Ishan Chandra Mustafi were two permanent Members of Raj shabha. The State jurisdiction was divided into ***'Civil'*** and ***'Criminal'*** which were represented by Courts, such as; *Sadr Amin, Dewani Ahilkar* and Appeal on the one hand and Naib Ahilkar and Sessions Ahilkar on the other hand, W.W.Hunter remarked that "the cases were tried in much the same manner as in our provinces, and the '*Amals*' were not inferior in capacity to the same officers like the courts elsewhere".[65]

British Government formed the 'State Council' in 1883 for interference in the internal administration in Cooch Behar State. The Government also prepared the Memorandum of administration.[66] The State Council was established with His Highness as president, other three members, namely, the Superintendent of the State, a Dewan and a Judicial Officer. Judicial Department was under direct control over the Superintendent of the State or Vice President of State Council of Cooch Behar State.

A. Criminal Justice

W.T. Smith, Deputy Commissioner had been given in his Annual Report for 1872–1873 regarding the history of constitution of the Criminal courts in the State – "It seems probable that justice was dispensed by the Raja or as Minister in primitive fashion as late as 1791; for when Mr. Douglas, Commissioner took charge of Cooch Behar in that year to look the administration of Civil and Criminal justice. The civil and criminal courts of original jurisdiction, the court of the Dewani Ahilkar and that of the Fouzdari Ahilkar appear to have been constituted when the British authority withdrew from interference in the internal affairs of Cooch Behar and were doubtless in immitation of the Maffusil Courts of the East India Company. Hindu Law was referred to in both civil and criminal cases, but the Regulations naturally had a powerful influence, beings the only modern laws known to the Bengali law who administered the affairs of the Raj".[67] The British Commissioners had found that judge was at liberty in disregard both the pundit's suggestion and the doctrine of the Hindu code.[68]

When Maharaja Nripendra Narayan came into power in 1864, the British Commissioner being monopolised by a great extent by the Bhutan expedition, on extensive change were made in the administration of Criminal justice. The **'Raj Sabha'** was transferred to the Commissioner's Office.[69] The constitution and procedure of the session court were same as early and session judge was appointed from the state and two additional Naib Ahilkars were appointed to the Fouzdari Court. During the minority of Maharaja Nripendra Narayan, the British Commissioner played the main role and the Commissioner controlled all the Departments. "In 1866, the Indian Penal Code and the code of criminal procedure were introduced by an order of the officiating Commissioner the details of office work and procedure were revised and corrected; the native sessions judge was removed; the duties of the Civil and sessions judge were added on to those of the Deputy Commissioner; the old Fouzdari Ahilkar was pensioned office replaced by a more competent man and a greatly improved status things began". [70]

During 3rd March, 1866, first Sub-division of the State was established in Tufanganj and the Assistant Fauzdari Ahilkar was placed in-charge. Firstly, the Sub-divisional Officer had functioned only Criminal jurisdiction. But 1868, he worked both in civil and Criminal departments. The second Naib Ahilkar was reappointed and he exercised both civil and criminal powers. In 1872, four additional sub-divisions were established in the muffasil because of the introduction of the *Khas Collection* system in the Revenue Department. The Sub-divisional Naib Ahilkar exercised civil and criminal powers within their respective jurisdictions.

Some changes however, came when Indian Criminal procedure code of 1872 (Act. X of 1872) was introduced in the State on September, 1873. On the introduction of that code, the practice and procedure of criminal courts were to be guided by that enactment with certain modifications. The sub-divisional Officers had the powers of sub-ordinate Magistrate of the first class under the code, but had no jurisdiction in the proceedings.[71] Sub-divisional Naib Ahilkars were empowered in 1875.

The administration of Cooch Behar State was carried on by the Maharaja, assited by a Council, consisting of three Members, namely, the Superintendent of the State, the Dewan or Chief Revenue Officer and the civil Judge. The Superintendent of the state supervised the administration of criminal justice and the police, military, jail, public works, education and Audit departments. He was also the session Judge, hearing all criminal appeals which ordinarily lay to session Judges in British districts.[72]

The Bengal Cattle Trespan Act (Act III of 1857) was acted in Cooch Behar State from the very early time. In 1850, the Raja-sabha had prohibited gambling. The Gamling Act, (Act 11 of 1867 B.C.) was ordered in the courts of the State in June 1870.[73] The Indian Evidence Act (Act I of 1872) was introduced in Cooch Behar in May 1873.[74] In Cooch Behar State all act was prepared in the direction of British Government. Formerly, no diary of witnesses in criminal cases was kept. In January, 1866 the system of keeping a register of the examination of witnesses was introduced. Before the introduction of the criminal procedure code the witnesses received no money, not even in session's cases.

Formerly, the Rajganj or the Kinsmen of the Maharajas did not appear to have been subject to the Jurisdiction of the criminal courts of the State. In August 1871, owing to a disorderly behaviour of a principal Rajganj, Colonel Haughton extended the jurisdiction of the deputy Commissioner to the trial of offences committed by a Rajganj under certain restriction. In 1892-93, [75] the jurisdiction of the Fauzdari Ahilkar was extended to the trial of *"Summons cases"* against the Rajganj. Five years later, in 1897-98,[76] this privilege of the Rajganj was asthdraun and Highness was pleased to order that in criminal cases no distinction should in future be made between Rajganjs and other persons.

In Cooch Behar State, common enamies in early times were dacoity and burglary. There were no doubts that the State, the absence of an organized system of police and lack of proper justice were the main reason for crimes. Other crimes were domestic violence and disputes over land. W.T. Smith (Deputy Commissioner of Cooch Behar State) "gives some statistics which are valuable, as enabling to compare the State of Cooch Behar in his time as regards to prevalence of crime not only with its present state but also what then existed in the neighbouring district of Jalpaiguri".[77] The table is given the figures of cognizable and non-cognizable offences reported for selected years from 1876-77 to 1947. It will be seen that from 1876 to 1947 the population had increased more than double but interestingly there had been no appreciable increase in the number of cognizable offences. The number of non-cognizable offences also remained almost the same till 1945.

TABLE –4.1

The figures of Cognizable and non-Cognizable Offences (1876 – 1950)

Year	*Number of cognizable offences*	*Number of non-cognizable offences*	*Total*
1876-77	1644	1465	3109
1901-02	1366	1182	2548
1902-03	1481	1306	2787
1903-04	1490	1474	2964
1904-05	1609	1517	2126
1921-22	1530	1110	2640
1922-23	1446	1106	2552
1923-24	1350	1018	2368
1927-28	1704	1136	2840
1928-29	1730	1172	2902
1929-30	1794	1180	2974
1933-34	1454	841	2295
1934-35	1627	949	2573
1949-50	2274	1024	3298

Source: 1951 Census Report, Cooch Behar District Hand Book, p. 64.

B. Police

Before British, there was only one Court in Cooch Behar for the trial of all kinds of cases and the court exercised powers in the name of the Maharja. There was no police station or system in Cooch Behar State.[78] After concluding the Anglo-Cooch Behar treaty, in 1773, the British Government tried to interfere in the internal administration of Cooch Behar. It may be noted, 1803 the post of the Commissioner of Cooch Behar was revived and Francis Pierard was appointed Commissioner of Cooch Behar for the purpose of carrying into effect, in concent with the Maharaja, certain necessary arrangements for the collection of the public revenue and the administration of justice and for the adoption of a proper and efficient system of police.[79] One of the most important objective was by the British Commissioners to reform the police force of the State. But the opposition of Maharaja Harendra Naryan, this objective was not carried out satisfactorily by any of them. Although Ahmuty (Commissioner of Cooch Behar State) established two *Thanas* in the interior of the State.

During the minority period of Maharaja Nripendra Narayan the new police force was established in 1866 by Colonel Bruce.[80] Captain Hedayat Ali was for some time in charge of the police. Moulavee Anwarooj Zaman, an Inspector of the Bengal constabulary was appointed the head of the Cooch Behar police. In the year 1866-67, the organisation of the new police was in full force and appeared to have been completed.[81]

The new Police force was formed consisting of one Inspector four Sub-Inspectors, twenty six Head Constables and two hundred Constables. In 1876-77, the number of police stations and out posts were extended.

TABLE 4.2

The Number of Police stations and Outposts in Cooch Behar State

Police station	*Outposts*
Kotwali	Khoita
Tufanganj (Afterwards called Fulbari)	Bhaishkuchi
Dinhata	Keshoribari
Mathabhanga	Shitalkuchi
Mekhliganj	Ksheti (Moranga)
	Kotebhajni
	Haldibari

Source: H. N. Chaudhury, *Cooch Behar State and its Land Revenue Settlement*, Cooch Behar, 1903, p. 309.

The police force was reorganised in 1876-1877 and it comprised of one Superintendent, three Inspectors, eight Sub-Inspectors, twenty-six head constables and two hundred and forty constables. The town or Municipal police was organized in 1885, consisting of one ***Jemadar*** and twenty-three ***Chowkidars*** for the town of Cooch Behar. The Municipal police was under the Superintendent of police.

C. Rural Police

Before 1875, there was nothing any rural police or Chowkidars in Cooch Behar State. The British Commissioner Colonel Haughton introduced the ***Chowkidari*** system to protect the villagers and their property. In 1882-83, fifteen hundred and seventy six ***Chowkidars*** were in the State. The Cooch Behar ***Chowkidari*** Act was passed in 1893-94.[82] The number of ***Chowkidars*** in the State came up to fourteen hundred seventy seven at the end of 1899-1900.

D. Cooch Behar Jail

A Jail for the custody of prisoners had been in existence from a very old time. Formerly it was two distinct departments; civil and criminal. When the commissioner took charge of the Cooch Behar State the old jail having fallen out of repair a new *kutcha* one was built to the south of the Sagardighi in 1864.[83] In 1874, a proposal for the building of a *pucca* wall was taken up and the bill for the same was sanctioned. The deputy Commissioner was in change of making the buildings *pucca* before constructing a masonry wall. The idea of making the wards of masonry had, however to be given up on grounds, and only the guard-house, the office, was built of masonry. A brick wall was constructed by prison labours; it was completed in 1879-80.[84] A Tank inside the jail was completed with jail labours in 1880. This tank supplied pure water to the prisoners.

A Jail garden was opened in 1868, and the Jail authority gave employments to those prisoners who were unfit for hard labour. The mark system for the regulation of the conduct of the convicts was introduced in 1873. The jail code of Bengal was followed in the management of the jail and Lock-ups were in the State. The Fauzdari Ahilkar was in charge of the jail, and was assisted by a Jailor and one Assistant Jailor.

The Cooch Behar jail was remarkable for its healthiest. Sir Stuart Bayley, Lieutenant Governor of Bengal, who visited Cooch Behar in 1889, was pleased to remark, "that the prisoner seemed to be well fed properly cared for." Prisoners were transferred from Cooch Behar State to Andaman Jail for British Government's own arrangement.

E. Lock-Ups

In the beginning, there was no separate building for the lock-ups and the prisoners were used to be kept in the *Thana* buildings. Subsequently regular lock-ups were built with the *Thana* guard house in their front, and a high bamboo wall covering the remaining sides. The lock-ups had separate cells for male and female prisoners. The first lock-up was opened at Dinhata in the state in 1870. Gradually the lock-ups were increased and those were under the management of the Sub-divisional officer.

4.3 Mobilisation of western culture-Education, health and Urbanisation

A. Education

Before going into details about the education policy of the Raj, It can be said that the dynasty which was founded by Viswa Singha was absolutely backward in education. During the time of Maharaja Nara Narayan this dynasty became most powerful but he could not make progress in the sphere of education. The early rulers of the dynasty only encouraged Sanskrit based education. They patronised the scholars with profound knowledge in Sanskrit literature. One of the main features during this time was that education was restricted to elite class and not for the masses or common people of the State. The education for the common people had its beginning during the reign of Maharaja Bir Narayan. He was a great patron of learning and established schools in various parts of his kingdom.[85] Among the later rulers Pran Narayan, though interested in education and patronised Sanskrit scholars and pandits, could not popularize education among the masses. Till the 19th century one may experience the slow progress in the field of education in Cooch Behar.

During the minority of Maharaja Narendra Narayan Bhup Bahadur, a vernacular school was started in the town of Cooch Behar in 1857, for the education of the children of Royal blood.[86] This may be said to be the first step taken towards popular education in the State. Thus the establishment of the Sadar M. E. School sowed the seed of popular learning in the State. In 1861 Mharaja Narendra Narayan offered a purse to Colonel Jenkins, Governnor General's Agent in the North East Frontier in recognition of the good services done by the Colonel during the minority of the Maharaja Nripendra Narayan. The worthy Colonel tactfully avoided accepting the reward and suggested that the money would be spent for a good cause if an English school were founded with that money. Accordingly, an English school was founded in 1861 and named Jenkins

School in honour of Colonel Jenkins. In the beginning it taught up to the third class of the entrance curriculum and later it received the recognition of the Calcutta University and sent up the first batch of five boys for the entrance Examination in 1870 of whom three passed.[87] In 1864, three other vernacular schools were opened in the interior and Ramchandra Ghosh, a State official was appointed Honorary Inspector of schools in addition to his other duties. Since 1865 the supervision of the schools was placed in the hands of a local Committee of public Instruction, assisted by the Government Inspector of schools of the North East Division.[88] In 1870 the member of village vernacular schools went up to 58 of which 5 were meant for girls. A Madrasa for teaching Persian and three Sanskrit tols were also started.

The gradual spread of education and extension of schools in the interior, the need or a separate whole time Superintendent of education was felt and in 1870, R. Robinson was appointed to be the first Superintendent of education in the State. In the next year, Kasikantha Mukharjee resigned from the Bengal Education service and joined the Superintendent of education of Cooch Behar State. A network of schools and pathsalas covered the entire State and for proper supervision, the establishment of the Superintendent of Education was strengthened between 1876 and 1878 by the additional Deputy Inspector of schools, and Sub Inspector of schools and four inspecting Pandits.[89]

According to G.J.B. Juite Dalton, the Deputy Commissioner of Cooch Behar prepared Annual Administrative Report of the State for 1876-77 was worth noting "There is no feature of our administration of the Cooch Behar State, on which we are entitled to look with greater satisfaction than the success which has attended our efforts in the cause of education. A very few years ago there was hardly a school in the Raj and very few except the *Muktears* or *Mohajans* could even read or write. At present Cooch Behar is ahead of Rangpur, Julpigoree (Jalpaiguri) and of all the Assam districts and can compare not unfavourably with some of the more advanced districts of lower Bengal. During the year under review the number of schools had increased from 282 to 323 and their pupil's from 7,238 to 7795 and the average daily attendance from 6087 to 7151. Five boys sent up from the State for the University entrance examination four passed and two of then won first grade junior scholarship. A scholar from the Raj passed the first Arts examination for the first time and another final examination of the medical school. At the minor scholarship competitive examination a native of Cooch Behar secured the second place in the general list. At the vernacular scholarship examination in competition with Assam, Cooch Behar passed as many candidates as three of Assam districts together. At the general examination of the normal schools in the lower provinces, Cooch Behar passed eight candidates against one for the neighbouing district of Rangpur. I mention these facts to show that while every year is swelling the numbers in our schools and increasing the percentage of our school going population, the quality of instruction imparted will compare favourably with the Goverment standard attained to in the neighbouring British districts". [90]

Lieutenant Governor of Bengal expressed here that large sum of money should be spent to this head for the multiplification of primary Schools. So State budget enhanced the allocation, and a number of primary Schools increased considerably. In the year 1879-80, 323 Schools, 7 were run entirely at State expense; Jenkins was the only one High English School, 2 middle vernacular Schools, two normal Schools, one Boarding School and one Artizen School. Two hundred and thirty one were Aided Schools. There were Middle English Schools 3, Middle vernacular Schools 88, lower vernacular Schools 96, Girls Schools 24, Night Schools 19, Boarding Schools 1, 13 Maktabs and the total expenditure of education was Rs. 74516 of which the States share was Rs. 49, 526.[91] In June, 1888 the first College was established in Cooch Behar named Victoria College to commemorate the Jublee of Queen Victoria of England.[92] This college was considered as a first grade College with

Arts upto BA standard and was affiliated to Calcutta University and science upto law Intermediate Course. Gradually the MA and the Law courses were opened and the college became one of the leading institutions in North Eastern India.

The budget for the primary Educaion and Secondary Education was separated from 1891 and by effecting savings in the primary sector where more of people's Cooch Behar was seemed.[93] In Cooch Behar State, education made considerable progress and the Table is shown, Primary and secondary stages.

TABLE –4.3

Total Number of Institutions, Students and Expenditure (1800 – 1947)

Year	*No. of Institutions*	*Total No. of Students*	*Total expenditures*
1800-1881	323	7795	35287
1890-1891	328	10242	39123
1900-1901	344	11519	40335
1910-1911	341	12913	57635
1920-1921	328	12367	76280
1930-1931	342	12933	91628
1940-1941	345	16443	119527
1947	360	18200	125620

Source: *Annual Administrative Report of Cooch Behar State*, Relevant Years.

The progress of education in the state compared with the neighbouring British districts. The population of Cooch Behar State was 5,66,973, of which 3,01,380 were males. The details are given below:-

TABLE – 4.4

Education in the State Compared with the Neighbouring British Districts

Districts	*Total male population*	*Male pupils of school going*	*No. of pupils at school*	*Percentage*
Rajshaye	717947	107691	19386	18.0
Dinajpur	774380	116157	21752	18.7
Rangpur	1061812	159271	27970	17.6
Jalpaiguri	364659	54698	11239	20.5
Cooch Behar	301380	45207	11208	24.7

Source: *Annual Administrative Report of Cooch Behar State,* 1900-1901, p. 27.

The percentage of literate's people is given below:

TABLE – 4.5

Yearwise the percentage of Literate People

Year	*Male*	*Female*
1901	10.7	0.4
1911	13.4	0.6
1921	13.9	0.9
1931	11.3	1.2
1941	13.6	2.1
1951	23.2	5.3

Source: Durgadas Majumdar, *West Bengal District Gazetteers,* Koch Behar, 1977, p. 177.

The education for the female deserves special mention; it was previously restricted to the ladies of the palace. But during the reign of Maharaja Nripendra Narayan education for the women received a special preference. In 1881 a land-marking step had been taken for the favour of women education in the State.[94] The Girl's school named Sunity Academy was established in the Capital town by the direct patronage of Maharani Sunity Devi. Gradually, the girl's schools were also established in the subdivision of the State.

A detail of the girls schools and their achievements are presented here to understand the success rate of the female education of the State-

TABLE – 4.6

Total number of Girsl Schools and Success Rate of Girls Students

Years	*Total No. of Girls Schools*	*Success Rate*
1870-71	6	-
1880-81	23	-
1890-91	10	-
1900-01	9	70.1%
1910-11	22	81.8%
1920-21	21	100%
1930-31	22	93.8%
1940-41	24	94.3%

Source: A. Bhattacharjee, *Madhuparni Special Issue of Cooch Behar*, 1990, pp. 208-209.

The education was extended to all classes of the society; Nripendra Narayan had a secular vision in spreading education to the grass roots. The secular attitude of the Maharajas of Cooch Behar in respect of education may be enumerated.

B. Health

Before the year 1819, the European system of medicine was unknown in Cooch Behar State.[95] The Rajas of Cooch Behar had found from early times ***Kavirajas*** *or Ayurvedic Physicians*. But this form of treatment was confined to the Royal family and to the upper classes. There were a large number of people who by and large had faith in *ojhas or* ***village quacks***. In June, 1814, the Commissioner, Macleod applied to the British Government to send a qualified medical man to the State but due to paucity of such man the Government was unable to send a single candidate as per the demand.[96] In 1819 an Indian doctor was sent to Cooch Behar on a salary of Rs. 40 per month but there was no record as to what his qualification or training was. In 1841 Maharaja Sibendra Narayan applied to the British Government for a qualified medical man and in February, 1842 Dr. Syama Charan Sarkar, a graduate of the Medical college of Calcutta was appointed Medical officer of the Maharaja's Court.[97] In 1846, the Maharaja asked for a European Medical officer and Dr. Ralph Moore was appointed Medical officer of the Maharaja.[98]

There was no attempt to open any Hospital or dispensary in Cooch Behar State before 1842, when Colonel Haughton took over charge of the administration during the minority of Maharaja Nripendra Narayan. The first dispensary was opened in Cooch Behar in the charge of a Sub-Assistant Surgeon in 1865. In 1869-70, the Medical establishment consisted of a Sub-Assistant Surgeon, two unqualified Doctors and four compounders.[99] At that time, there were other three Hospitals at the sudder, the police, Military and jail. The Sub-Assistant Surgeon was incharge of the Medical Department upto May, 1873, when the post of the Civil Surgeon was created and Dr. Thomas Briscoe was appointed to it. Henceforth the Assistant Surgeon came to be incharge of Dispensary only.

The first dispensary to be opened in the mofussil was on 13th June, 1873 at Dinhata. The Mekhliganj dispensary was opened on 9th August, 1874 and the Mathabhanga dispensary on 28th September, 1874. Arrangement for in patients was made in both these dispensaries in 1875-76.[100] There was at this time no qualified Medical Graduate or licentiate incharge of the Subdivisional dispensaries or Hospitals. In 1885, Haldibari dispensary was opened for the treatment of outpatients. A dispensary was started at Fulbari in 1888-89.[101]

In 1866-67, the number of patients was treated at the Hospitals and Dispensaries. The number gradually increased as shown below:-

TABLE – 4.7

The number of Inpatients and Outpatients in Cooch Behar State

Year	*Inpatients*	*Outpatients*	*Total*
1880-81	1289	13236	14525
1890-91	1487	16998	18485
1900-01	1332	19890	21222
1910-11	1149	39460	40609
1920-21	1689	48346	50035
1930-31	1527	58515	60042
1940-41	2708	169261	171969
1950-51	304	20522	20826

Source: H.N. Chaudhury, *Cooch Behar State and its Land Revenue Settlement*, Cooch Behar, 1903, p.338.

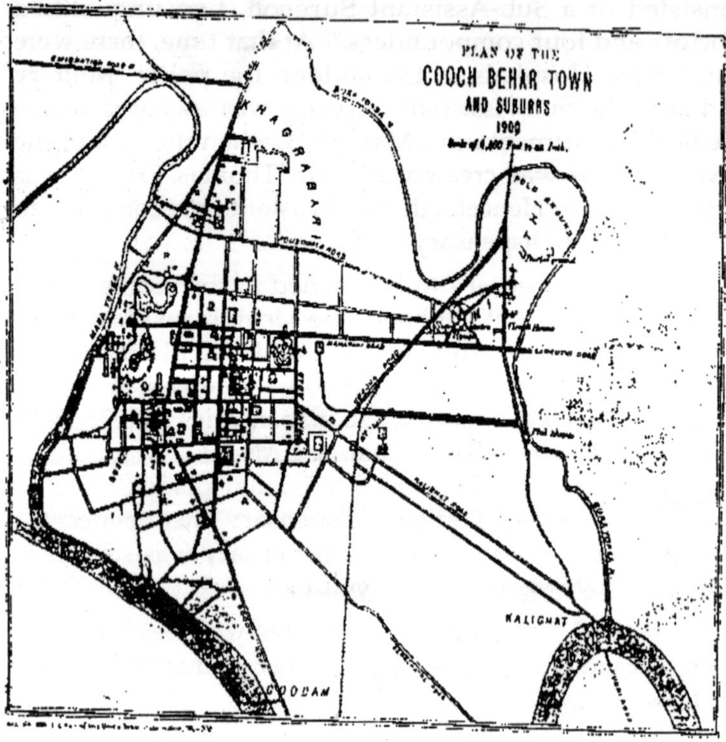

These dispensaries and hospitals were established near the state head quarters and at the sub divisional head quarters and were visited mainly by the people of the towns and those living close by. The rural people remained apathetic to the scientific treatment and still had faith in ***ojhas and village quaks***. The principal diseases of the people attending the dispensaries and hospitals were fever, spleen, Rheumatic affections, skin diseases and goiter etc.

In 1865-66, the vaccination was the only preventive against small pox. Colonel Haughton the Commissioner secured the services of some vaccinators from the Government of Bengal during 1869-71. The following figures give a picture of the progress of vaccination in the State between 1873 to 1941.

TABLE 4.8

Total Number of vaccinated Persons (1873–1941)

Years	*Number of persons vaccinated*
1873-1874	4449
1880-1881	17447
1890-1891	13755
1900-1901	16895
1910-1911	45017
1920-1921	31193
1930-1931	12529
1940-1941	65764

Source: Durgadas Majumdar, *West Bengal District Gazetteers*, Koch Behar, 1977, pp.182-183.

The statement below shows the birth and death statistics with their respective rates per thousand of population during the year of 1900 to 1940.

TABLE – 4.9

Percentage of birth and death statistics with respective rates in Cooch Behar (1900 –1941)

Year	*Birth rates*	*Death rates*
1900-01	18.45	25.43
1910-11	16.32	15.40
1920-21	18.23	15.30
1930-31	13.28	1162
1940-41	26.81	2264

Source: *Annual Administrative Report of Cooch Behar State*, Relevant Years.

Thomas Briscoe was the first civil Surgeon of Cooch Behar State and assumed the charge of Medical Officer of the State in 1873. Surgeon Major H. Coopeson officiated in the post till 1877. Dr. Henry holds the post till 1892. Gradually the post was held by one and another European doctors. The European modern medicine system gradually improved the health system of Cooch Behar. The people of Cooch Behar, mainly Maharaja of State wanted and requested to the British Government for European style of treatment.

C. Urbanisation

Evolution of towns-that is the origin, development and changing character, function and morphology of town is a fascinating subject of study. This is not only a matter of historical interest; one finds, there are trends in development leading from the past to the present.[102] All of we know that in the late Nineteenth Century, Britain had become the most highly urbanized Nation of the World, though North West Europe which had fed the cities, spilled over into the great migratory flows. Which took European people to the World under-developed regions of the World.[103] By contrast, in those areas of the World in Africa, Asia, and the Far East, which had been seized by the great powers in the scamble for Empire, the rate of urbanization, though significant for commercial and capital cities was over all very much lower.

The urban areas of this State had also grown at a lesser rate than that observed in the urban West Bengal as a whole. Ofcourse, during 1911-1921, urban West Bengal registered an increase of 7-16 percent while urban Cooch Behar showed an increase of 4.29%. During the first twenty years of the 20th century, Cooch Behar showed a beter growth rate of population than the State of West Bengal as a whole. In the Cooch Behar State an increase of population by 4.5% was registered against the West Bengal State's growth of 3.15%. The urban population in 1901 as 100 the index of urban growth had been calculated both for State of West Bengal and State for,the Cooch Behar as following:-

TABLE – 4.10

Growth of Urban Populatin compares between Cooch Behar and West Bengal (1901-1951)

YEARS	*WEST BENGAL*	*COOCH BEHAR*
1901	100	100
1911	114	112
1921	122	123
1931	140	128
1941	229	191
1951	304	357

Source: Durgadas Majumdar, *West Bengal District Gazetteers*, Koch Behar, 1977, p. 107.

The whole of the State was parcelled out into ***Moujas***, closely resembling the modern taluk and there were grouped under the wider Sub-divisions of Zillas, *Toks* and *Gerds* Ahumity's (Commissioner of Cooch Behar) Quinquennial register of 1799, different Mouzas. There were then four Zillas-Gitaldah, Mathabhanga, Durga nagar and Lalbazar, one *Tok* of Mekhliganj and four Gerd-Patchara, Teldhar, Uchalpukhari and Maraghat.[104] The Sub-divisional system of administration was not adopted before 1870, in which year after the conclusion of O Donel's survey, each of the six Parganas was constituted into a district Sub-division by Colonel Haughton.[105] The Muffassil Sub-divisions were of first concerned with the collection of revenue only; attached to them for the inconvience of the public.

British Government not only introduced regulation to develop the administration in favour of urbanization but also developed the communication system all over the State. Before Colonel Haugton's (1861) arrival in Cooch Behar State, the total road's lenth was fourty one ***milles***. All the roads started from Cooch Behar town and connected other parts of the State like – Baneswar, Balarampur, and Moghalhat etc. Dalton (Deputy Commissioner of Cooch Behar) gave a vivid account of the condition of roads, "there was literally destitute of the good roads for even cart-traffic when the Governnment assumed charge. Fair weather roads existed Colonel they were transected every few milles by rivers and water course which were unbridged and often lay through plaugh of rice cultivation which in the rainy season were impassable. The course of rivers themselves formed an out let for the trade of the country, but internal communication was tedious and difficult".[106] The British administration played an important role for communication improvement. From 1865 to 1876 was called great road making activity by the Britisha Government in Cooch Behar State. They constructed every main line of roads with straight, high and broad and village roads were also constructed. At the end of 1898-1899, there were five ***milles*** of metalled road, three hundred seventy six and half ***milles*** of unmetlled road and one hundred eighty seven milles of village roads of the State.[107] Before 1876 there was no Railways in Cooch Behar State. In 1876, the North Bengal Railway opened a station at Haldibari. The Gitaldah-Manshahi Railway line opened in 1893, followed by Manshahi Cooch Behar extention in 1898 and another extention from Cooch Behar Alipurduar in 1900. The Railway which later (1913-1914) came to be the Cooch Behar

State Railway and the Bengal Douars States Railway actually opened up a new vista of development of the State of Cooch Behar.

The Cooch Behar was a small State and total number of town was six, each of the five Sub-divisional Head Quarter was a town, though some of them were big village called town almost by courtesy. Some of the towns of this district even do not satisfy the basic qualifying tests laid down in the cencus for defining an urban area, except of course of their being administered by the town committee.

In Cooch Behar State, the State Head quarter town of Cooch Behar was a Municipality. There were other five towns each of which was administered by a town committee. In 1901 the State had four towns viz, Cooch Behar, Dinhata, Mthabhanga and Haldibari. Two other towns Tufanganj and Mekhliganj were incorporated in 1941.

NOTES AND REFERENCES

1. Dipak Kumar Chaudhuri, *The Political Agents and the Native Raj – Conflict, Conciliation and Progress in Tripura between 1871 to 1890*, p. 27.
2. *Loc.cit.*
3. I. Copland, *The British Raj and the Indian Princes*, Bombay, 1982, p. 57.
4. Amanatulla Ahmed, *Cooch Beharer Itihas* (Bengali), Cooch Behar, p. 373.
5. *Ibid.*, p. 416.
6. *Cooch Behar Select Records*, Vol. I, p. 47.
7. *Ibid.*, pp. 28–32.
8. S.C. Ghosal, *A History of Cooch Behar*, 1942, p. 345.
9. Joy Nath Munshi, *Rajupakhyan*, pp. 89–99.
10. H.N.Chaudhury, *The Cooch Behar State its Land Revenue Settlement*, 1903, p. 252.
11. Cooch Behar Select Records, Vol. 1, p. 30.
12. *Ibid.*, pp. 29–32.

13. Amanatulla Ahmed, *op.cit.*, p. 227.
14. *Ibid*, p. 228.
15. H.N. Chaudhury, *op.cit.*, p. 445.
16. Cooch Behar Select Records, Vol. I , p. 45.
17. *Ibid.*, p. 76.
18. *Ibid.*, p. 48.
19. *Ibid.*, p. 49.
20. *Ibid.*, p. 51.
21. *Ibid.*, p. 51.
22. Joy Nath Munshi, *op.cit.*, pp. 105-106.
23. *Ibid.*, pp. 99-100.
24. *Cooch Behar Select Records*, Vol. I, pp. 135-36.
25. *Ibid.*, pp. 89-90.
26. Letter from Government to Harendra Narayan, November 13, 1805 (CBSR) Vol. I, p. 120.
27. Letter from G. Dowdeswell (Chief Secretary of Government) to J. Digby, Commissioner of Cooch Behar 12th June, 1813, (CBSR),Vol. I, p. 140.
28. K.M. Panikkar, *Relations of Indian States with the Government of India*, p. 106.
29. Letter from G. Dowdeswell to J. Dibby (Commissioner of Cooch Behar) 12th June, 1813, (CBSR),Vol. I, p. 132.
30. Letter from J. Adam, (Secretary to the Govt.) to the Rajah of Cooch Behar 27th May, 1814,(CBSR), Vol. I, p. 152.
31. Harendra Narayan Chaudhury, *op. cit.*, p. 257.
32. Letter from J. Adam, secretary to Government to Norman Macleod, Commissioner of Cooch Behar, 24th February, 1816, (CBSR), Vol. I, p. 130.
33. *Ibid.*, p. 132.
34. Letter from F. Curric, Secretary to the Govt. of India to F. Jenkins, the Agent of the Governor General, N.E. Frontier, 19th March, 1845, (CBSR), Vol. II, p. 96.
35. *Ibid*, p. 98.

36. Letter from T.W. Maddak, Sectary to the Govt. of India to Captain Jenkins, Agent. Governor General N.E. Frontier, 15th March 1841.
37. Letter from Jenkins Agent, Governor General to G. A. Bushley, Esq. Secy. Govt. of India, 27th September, 1842.
38. *Cooch Behar Select Records*, Vol. I, p. 102.
39. *Ibid.,* p. 103.
40. *Loc.cit.*
41. *Loc.cit.*
42. Letter from secretary, Govt. of Bengal, to Government of India, Foreign Department, 14 December, 1848, (CBSR), Vol. II, p. 92.
43. *Ibid.,* p. 96.
44. *Ibid.,* 10th April, 1860, p. 104.
45. H.N. Chaudhury, *op.cit.,* p. 287.
46. *Cooch Behar Select Records*, Vol-II, p. 235.
47. *Ibid,* p.276.
48. Dalton's Retrospective Sketch of Government Administration of Cooch Behar, p. 8.
49. H.N. Chaudhury, *op.cit.,* p. 278.
50. No. 25561, dated 12th August, 1885, Simla.
51. *Annual Administrative Report of Cooch Behar State,*1903–1904, p. I.
52. *Ibid.,* 1912 – 1913, p. 6.
53. *Ibid.,* p. 7.
54. *Ibid.,* p. 8.
55. *Ibid.,* 1936-1937, p. 8.
56. H. N. Chaudhury, *op.cit.,* pp. 296-98.
57. *Loc. cit.*
58. S. N. Sen, *Prachin Bengal Patra Sankalan* (A collectior of letters in Bengali), p. 21.
59. Cooch Behar Select Records, Vol. I, Para. 52-53.
60. *Ibid,* pp. 133-135.
61. *Loc. cit.*

62. *Loc. cit.*
63. *Ibid,* pp. 321-325.
64. S. N. Sen, Letter No. 131, p. 58.
65. W. W. Hunter, *A Statistical Account of Bengal,* Vol. X, p. 427.
66. H. N. Chaudhury, *op.cit.,* p.290.
67. *Annual Administrative Report of Cooch Behar State,* 1872–1873, p. 27.
68. H. N. Chaudhury, *op.cit.,* p. 291.
69. *Annual Administrative Report of Cooch Behar State,* 1865, p. 30.
70. H. N. Chaudhury, *op.cit.,* p. 304.
71. *Annual Administrative Report of Cooch Behar State,* 1872–1873, p. 35.
72. W. W. Hunter, *The Imperial Gazetteer of India,* Vol. VIII, Karens to Madnagarh, 2nd Edition, 1886, pp. 325-327.
73. *Annual Administrative Report of Cooch Behar State,* 1870, p. 39.
74. *Ibid.,* 1873, p.42.
75. *Ibid.,* 1892-1893, p. 30.
76. *Ibid.,* 1897-1898, p. 25.
77. Cooch Behar Select Records, Vol. I, p. 131.
78. *Ibid.,* p. 132.
79. H. N. Chaudhury, *op.cit.,* pp. 310-311.
80. *Ibid,* p. 309.
81. *Annual Administrative Report of Cooch Behar State* ,1876-77, p. 5.
82. *Ibid.,* 1893-94, pp. 6-7.
83. *Ibid.,* 1896, p. 132.
84. *Ibid.,* p. 8.
85. S. C. Ghosal, *op.cit.,* p. 168.
86. Durgadas Majumdar, *op.cit.,* p. 174.
87. *Annual Administrative Report of Cooch Behar State,* 1870-71, p. 16.

88. *Proceedings of the Government of Bengal,* Judicial (Political), Department, April, 1872.
89. H. N. Chaudhury, *op.cit.,* pp. 215-216.
90. *Annual Administrative Report of Cooch Behar State,* 1876-77, pp. 34-35.
91. *Ibid.,* 1879-80, pp. 33-34.
92. *Ibid.,* 1888-1889, p. 36.
93. *Government of West Bengal: Census 1961, West Bengal District Census Hand Book, Cooch Behar,* p. 120.
94. *Female Education in Bengal,* Calcutta, 1936, p. 132.
95. H. N. Chaudhury, *op.cit.,* p. 337.
96. *Cooch Behar Select Records,* Vol. II, 1888, p. 132.
97. *Ibid,* p. 140.
98. S. C. Ghosal, *op.cit.,* p. 342.
99. Durgadas Majumdar, *op.cit.,* pp. 182-183.
100. *Annual Administrative Report of Cooch Behar State,* 1875-1876, p. 34.
101. *Ibid,* 1888-89, p. 36.
102. K.V. Sundaram, *Urban and regional planning in India,* Delhi, 1977, p. 145.
103. K.N. Chaudhuri, C.S. Dewey (ed), *Economy, Society, of India,* Delhi, 1979, p. 330.
104. H.N. Chaudhury, *op.cit.,* p. 326.
105. *Ibid,* p.327.
106. *Annual Administrative Report of Cooch Behar State,* 1864-1865, p. 12.
107. Durgadas Majumdar, *op.cit.,* p. 116.

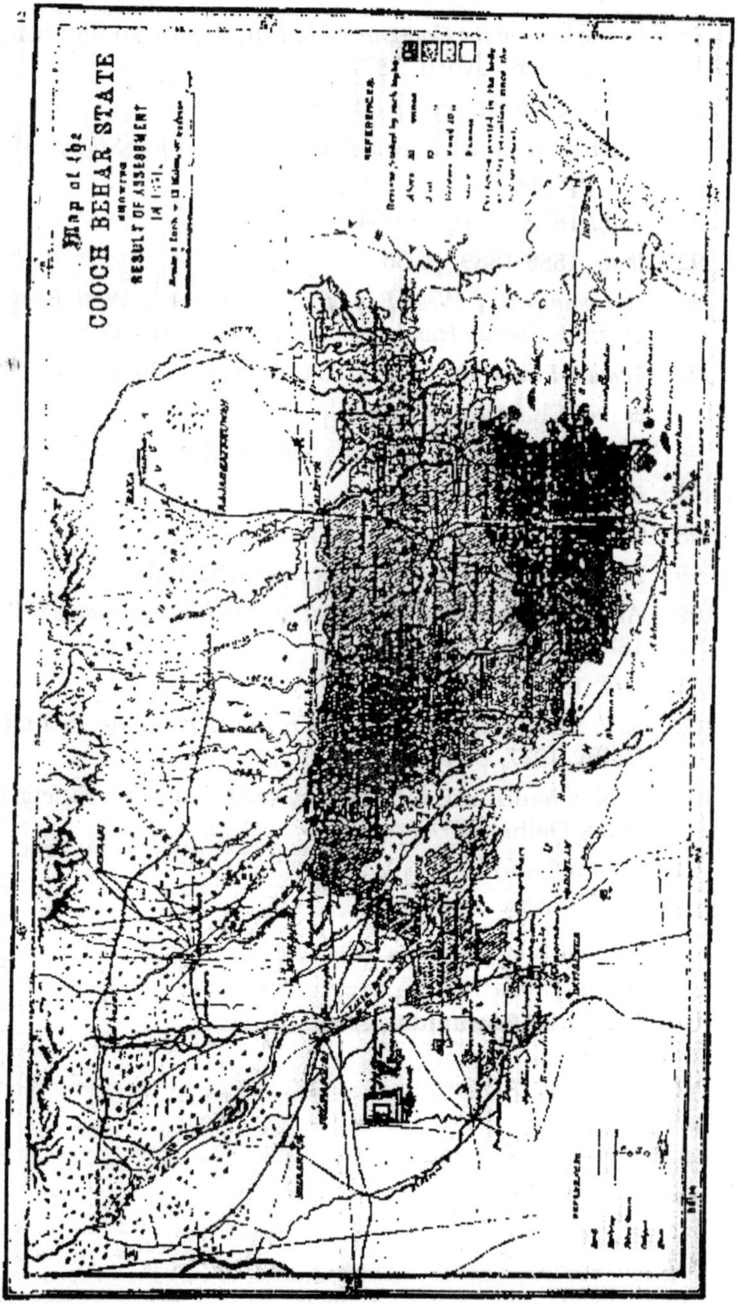
Map of the
COOCH BEHAR STATE
SHOWING
RESULT OF ASSESSMENT

5

Anatomy of Revenue Administration

The Principal sources of revenue of princely State of Cooch Behar were as under -

5.1 Land Revenue

5.2 Stamp Revenue

5.3 Revenue from the Forest Products

5.4 Excise Revenue

5.5 Revenue from other Sources

From the available documents it appears that in 1773 the annual revenue derived from all the above mentioned sources were amounted to Rs 1,99,120 in Narayani *Coins*.[1] But surprisingly in 1790, the revenue collection reduced to Rs. 1,19,946 in Narayani coins when British Commissioner Henry Douglas took over charge of the Cooch Behar State. According to British Commissioner the deficit of revenue resulted from the mal-administration of the Raja's Minister who had not only himself been guilty of the greatest oppressions, but had also connived at then in his deperndents and large portions of lands had been alienated. As a result, many new taxes were introduced. So, harassed and oppressed, many Ryots left the State. During 1790 A.D. the gross amount of the revenues[2] of the *Chaklahs* of Bodah, *Khas Mehals* were as follows—

Behar Narayani Rs.........	1,19,946	11	16	1
Or Sicca Rs..................	88,034	4	17	0
Bodah and C: Arcot Rs.......	1,06,085	7	14	1
Or Rs..........................	97,103	6	13	0
Khas Mehals : Narayani Rs...	1,100	0	0	0
Or Arcot Rs..................	9,769	14	6	3
Total =	**1,94,887**	**12**	**2**	**0**

In these circumstances, Henry Douglas introduced some reforms, which helped to increase the revenue of the Cooch Behar State. The main objective of the British Government was to collect money and to stabilize economic condition of the State. Henry Douglas completed the first ever settlement report under his direct supervision.[3] There after, various reformative measures were taken by the successive British Commissioners' for developing the revenue administration and revived the moribund economy of the Cooch Behar State.

5.1 Land Revenue

It is very essential to understand the general economic condition of the state of Cooch Behar before the time of the British East India Company. The economy of the state rested on agriculture but nothing definite could be known about the system of land tenure, mode of assessment of revenue, total quantity of land or its distribution till the British had made a probe into these.[4] From the very early times, the lands were divided into two kinds A. Revenue paying lands B. Rent free lands. In the case of the First kind of lands, tenants had to pay revenue to the State. The rent-free land was held by the State for special purposes. These lands were given as reward to the performers of religious rites, learned man and Brahmins, for their service to the State. The private individuals who obtained such lands for special purposes and enjoyed them free of any charges as ***Debutter, Brahmatter, Lakharaj*** and ***Petbhata*** according to the purposes for which these were allotted.[5]

Lands were also granted to persons for doing personal service to the state, and they were called *Jaigirs*.

A. **Debutter** grants were lands given for the support of an idol. These lands could not be sold or alienated in any way. There were two categories of such grants in Cooch Behar State. i) **State Debutter**: These *Debutter* grants were supervised directly by the officers of the State. The traditional pujas or worships were perfored under the guidanceof the state officers.

ii) **Private Debutter** Brahmins asked the Raja for a *Debutter* grant to support him to worship his own *idol*.

B. **Brahmatter** lands were given to Brahmans for their support to the State; such grants were hereditary and transferable.

C. **Lakheraj** lands were given to persons for doing some praise worthy work for the welfare of the state.

D. **Petbhata** lands were rent free lands given by the Raja for the maintenance of their relatives. The *Petbhata* grants applyed to the Raja were subject to renewal after the death of the owner.

Revenue paying lands were divided under ***Mal, Debutter*** and *Khangi*. *Mal* was available for state Revenue; the *Debuter* was sequestrated for religious purposes; and the *khangi* was set apart for the maintenance of the maharaja's household.[6] The persons colltecting and paying the charge on the land immediately to the state, or to the persons authorized to receive the same were called *Jotedars* and formed the first grade in the tenancy of the State.[7] Originally these men were perhaps the cultivatos of the soil and residents of the state, and the different grades of under tenure did not probably exist. When Charles Purling prepared the account of the Revenue of Cooch Behar in 1180 B.E. corresponding to 1774 A.D. he found that the Revenue payable by the *Rayat* consisted of two parts, viz. ***Asal*** or original rent and ***Abwab*** or additional cesses, which were consolidated into one. There was, however, no fixation of rent and regular pattas were not granted to the tenants. **The settlement** of land revenue was made annually, but the land was never measured and assessed. The system of collection of revenue and the mode of assessment were under no fixed rule.[8]

There were other categories of lands – ***Dewanbos, khasbos*** and ***Baje Mahal***.[9] *Mal* or khalsa land supported the Government's land property and the Dewan himself collected the revenue. 2%-3% of the total revenue was collected from the khalsa land. The *khangi* lands were officially applied to the demense lands of the Raja.[10] The fallow lands converted into cultivated lands were called ***Dewanbos***. ***Khasbos*** and ***Baje Mahal*** were the two branches of ***khangi Mahal***.[11]

In 1774, Charles Purling, Collector of Rangpur, prepared a ***Hust – o – Bood***[12] or account of the annual land Revenue of Cooch Behar. The amount of revenue exclusive of Jaigir and private land was 1, 99,120–3-0 – 15 Narayani rupees equivalent to Rs. 1,33,000 in modern currency. The revenue however, decreased in 1790 as mentioned earlier when Henry Douglas took over the charge of the Cooch Behar State. There after the protection of the British Government, the land revenue of the State gradually increased. Before the first settlement (1877) the land revenue amounted to Rs. 3,64,138–13–8. The detail is given below:-

TABLE – 5.1
Amount of Land Revenues

Name of parganas	*Mal/Khalsa*			*Debutter*			*Total*		
	Rs.	As.	P	Rs.	As.	P	Rs.	As.	P
Mekhliganj	52,932	5	2	1,835	12	1	54,768	1	3
Matabhanga	63,667	8	1	6,979	13	1	70,647	5	2
Lalbabar	73,234	6	11	1,241	12	2	74,476	3	1
Dinhata	72,282	9	5	4,168	4	2	76,450	13	7
Cooch Behar	59,949	14	5	11,570	8	8	71,520	7	1
Tufanganj	13,232	9	6	3,043	6	0	16,275	15	6
Total =	3,35,299	5	6	28,839	8	2	3,64,138	13	8

Source: H.N. Chaudhury, *Cooch Behar State and its Lands Revenue Settlement*, 1903, p. 569.

The Jotedars felt that the system of ***khas*** collection of revenue was in a sense a good system of revenue collection but Government was not well organized and could not realize the prospect of this system properly. It was found more convenient to farm out the revenue paying Estates to outsiders. But they did not carryout their responsibility of collecting revenue. "The country", observes Henry Douglas "Should be let out in small farms of one or more villages for the farm. The system of holding the lands ***khas*** appears to be attended with many disadvantages. Considering the extent of the country containing perhaps twenty or thirty thousand ***rayats,*** it is impossible for the proprietor or his manager to be intimately acquainted with the circumstances of every individual. He, therefore, cannot know when to assist the honest and industrious husbandman, and when to exact with rigour his revenue from the ***knavish*** rayat. Neither can he effectually superintend the conduct of the numerous officers required to collect the revenues directly from the rayats. Oppression may indeed be prevented, but it will be found impossible to discover frauds and collusion between these officers and the rayats. Besides, the officers have no interest in 'the improvement of the lands which will in consequence be neglected".[13] Henry Douglas (Commissioner of the Cooch Behar State) also noticed "many abuses and irregularities with regards to the land revenue system in Cooch Behar. There were too many taxes in the state. 1/3 of the whole revenue was consumed by those engaged in the collection of ***Mufussil khurcha*** and they were not shown in public accounts. ***Nazzars*** and ***Salamis*** were also to be paid by the rayats. Large portion of the lands had been in the possession of Sarbananda Gosain and Maharani enjoyed the whole of the Raja's private lands, the revenue of which amounted to Rs. 15,883 per year".[14]

In 1790, ***Ijardari*** system was introduced by Henry Douglas for land revenue collection in the State. The main objective was to secure the state revenue and ***khash*** collection. The modes of settlement adopted under this system were as follows –

1. The State was divided into lots of one or more villages each and these were put up to auction and the highest terms offered upon approved security were accepted. The ***jamas*** were agreed upon by the farmers used to make up the revenue, the same way as the revenue from ***Syrat Mehal*** was obtained in the same process.
2. The ***Jamas*** payable by the *jotedars* to these farmers were generally settled agreeably to that of preceding year. When the lands were measured, which was not very usually done, the farmers made their assessments according to certain fixed rates.
3. The settlement was at first made annually. During Richard Ahmuty's time the settlements were made for every five years.
4. As their authorized share of profit the ***Ijardars*** collected from the *rayats* two charges called ***Ijardari*** and ***Saranjami***, each forming one twelveth, and the two together one-sixth parts of the ***Jamas*** payable by the *rayats*.[15]

Seven years after the introduction of the ***Ijara*** system Ahmuty, the commissioner of the Cooch Behar state, wrote to the Governor General on the evil effects of the ***Ijara*** system thus – "The system adopted in former years was the mode to obtain the highest possible revenue for a short period, but it apperars from experience, ill calculated to promote the happiness of the people and the permanent prosperity of the country. Exclusive of the loss sustained by the proprietor the actual cultivators of the soil have suffered considerably from the lands being let at rack – rent to individuals, many of who could have no interest in their welfare and who availed themselves of every opportunity of extorting from them as much as possible. Consequently whole villages deserted and retired into adjacent districts of Rangpur and Dinajpur, were they found greater security and encouragement of their labour under established regulations of Government and a diference of more than seventy thousand of rupees was experienced in the *Jama* of year subsequent to *1201*".[16]

The ***Ijaradari*** system occupied a very important place in the revenue system of Cooch Behar. Most of land in this kingdom was farmed by some 100 to 125 ***Ijaradars***, who obtained farms at auctions held at the central office (Mal Kachari). Influential persons such as the queens (Ranis), members of the Royal family (kunwars or kuchwa sahibs), high-ranking officers and the spiritual guide (Guru) of the Raja usually secured the farms. They used to take out the *Ijaras benami* and by virtue of their position they could easily make exactions from the rayats. They got the best farms on easy terms, their influence prevented competition, and the deficiency in revenue was attempted to be made good by over assessing the farms held by others. But the only change Ahmuty brought about was to enhance the period of these farming leases to five years from one year as originally introduced by Henry Douglas.

There was no certainity of the tax being collected from the land and plough, but the Ijaradars took as much as they could get from the rayats, either by foul or fair means. The rayats had no means what so ever of complaining against the Queen, her children, Raja's ***Gurus*** and ***Umlahs*** "who hold land as Ijaradars .... and the creature who does complain is so harassed and distressed by them that his ruin is complete.........he is obliged to sell his all; plough – cattle and children; and when completely ruined, without food or clothes, he is at last obliged to run away to either the company's or Bhootan's dominions ....of course, the land vacated.....................runs to jungle ....on which account the revenue is lessened and indeed destroyed".[17]

Kalika Doss Dutt notes, "I can cite cases in which Ijraradars have turned entire talooks in to their own jotes. By sales for arrears of revenue or debts also, many jotes passed in to the hands of influential officers. There are paersons ....every one of whom holds about a hundred jotes or more. A jotedar now is not ....always the proprietor of one jote only .... To assertain what portion of the raj is held by foreign ***jotedars***. I referred to the settlement papers of 185 talooks already received by me. From calculation made, I found that out of about 1,50,000 ***beegahs*** of revenue-paying lands included in these talooks, about 81,000 beegahs are held by foreigners; of the remaining 69,000 beegahs, less than a third is held by cultivating jotedars, and the remainder by resident jotedars, who do not actually cultivate lands, but live on profits derived from Chookanidars". [18]

When Maharaja Harendra Narayan attained his maturity in 1801, the matter remained stuck up there. In subsequent years attempts were made by the British Government to introduce regulated administraton in the state but the refusal of the Maharaja prevented any further interference. Further improvement in revenue administration had to await another minority of the Raja in 1864.

Deputy Commissioner of Cooch Behar State William Smith gave a very vivid description of the rural society and the relationship between the jotedars and their under-tenants in his letter of 1872 - "There are no village headmen in Cooch Behar and with a few exceptions there are no villagers properly so called. The state has long been divided .... into talooks, the member of which is nearly 1200.............[The] taluk contains several square miles of country and many separate hamlets and collections of houses............Families living in this manner by themselves or in small hamlets have no need of chiefs like large communities, and no such persons exist."[19] He also records about the Jodtedars and writes, "Each jotedars, is master over his own projas or laborers, and he generally has then living on his premises. His chukanidars or under tenants also respect his authority to some slight extent. When the jotedar is a new resident, his position in the mofussil is occupied by chukanidar. Wealthy resident jotedars and chukanidars have some ascendancy and influence over their poorer reighbors, as well as over their dependents and many of them bear some little, such as Purdhan, Bosunia, Paramanik or (rarely) Mundul ....In some talooks there may be several persons bearing titles of this king, in others there may be a single person or none. In former times, when the administration of justice was less efficient, the bearers of these titles exercised rather more power than they do now. At present they have not much power. They are, however, often consulted be fore resort is had to the courts, and they have sufficient influence to settles of purdhan and Co, are generally hereditary, but the more title carries no influence with it..........in every house (baree) there is an individual called "dervania" chosen by the family ....to be a spokesman...........There are no established punchayets in any part of the state". [20] About the officers and mode of administration he again informs, "In some talooks there are people called patwarees, who write accounts and other documents, and make rough measurement ....if required. They have no fixed rename narration, but get a few annas from those who employ them.......patwarees are of no particular caste; they may be eiher Rajbungshees or Musalmans...........they do not, as a rule, collect rent for others. In most talooks there is an official, and in some other there are more than one called Hal Manjhee. He is a sort of pyada appointed by the jotedars and other ryos, and paid a small salary amounting to about one rupee a month. His duty is to carry instalment of rent to the izaradars or other receiver of rent and to bring back receipts for the same he also carries messages". [21]

The only effective remedy for all these evils was a general survey of the whole state and preparation of a Record of Rights of all the tenants from the jotedars downward and to determine the rents at each level. Colonel Haughton, the commissioner, accordingly applied to the Government of Bengal for the survey and O'Donnel, the Deputy superintendent of Revenue Department was specialy deputed by the Government for the purpose.[22] Before the survey was undertaken by O'Donnel a topographical survey of the state had been made by Pemberton, the superintendent of Revenue survey of the Government of Bengal in 1858. Pemberton's survey demarcated the boundaries of the state. The general topography of the State showing the position of the rivers, roads, towns, etc. was mapped. O'Donnel's survey measured the State in standard ***bighas*** of eighty cubits square (cubit=18 inches) and in ***kathas*** and ***dhurs***. The survey was made by the Company with a chain of 30 feet. O'Donnel divided the country into six ***parganas*** or circuits and within the ***parganas***, the *taluks* were geographically demarcated.[23] He was assisted by Iswar Chandra Sen, designated as a Deputy Collector.

The survey was concluded in 1870 and from 1872 under orders of Sir George Campbell, the Lieutenant governor of Bengal, the Ijaradari system was abolished and khas collection was introduced from 1st April of 1872. The collection ***tauzis*** were prepared by carefully putting together all the component parts of the jotes found by survey and by applying the accepted rate to these parts. The jotedars were to pay their revenue to the subdivisional kutcheries.[24] Default of payment entailed annulment of the patta, holding the jote, which was generally for thirty years though lesser periods were fixed in some cases. Later the Koch Behar Land Revenue Sales Act. was promulgated under provision of which defaulting jotes were to be put to auction and sold for arrears of revenue.

The British Government decided to do the settlement operations of Cooch Behar and for this reason W.O.A. Beckett was appointed Assistant Commissioner and he was assisted by five Deputy Collectors. The work of the first Land Revenue settlement of Cooch Behar was concluded in 1877. One important feature of the settlement operation was the resumption of the invalid rent free lands, ***Mokararis*** and ***jaigirs***, During the unsettled condition of the country beginning from the minority of Maharaja Harendra Narayan, large areas of land had been illegally alienated and turned into rent free land and jaigir Mahals by the clique in power.[25] All these cases were subjected to a close scrutiny during the settlement operations and those held invalid were resumed. The general rates adopted for the settlement were–

TABLE – 5.2

Details of General Rates adopted for the Settlement

Different type of lands	*Rs*	*As*	*P*
For homestead lands and gardens..... Per Bighas	2	8	0
For bamboo lands........... Per Bighas	1	2	0
For other cultivated lands includingThatching granlands and small bils			
Of less than 2 bighas.....per bighas	0	8	0
For fallow and jungle lands........per bighas	0	0	0

Source: H.N. Chaudhury, *Cooch Behar State and its Lands Revenue Settlement*, 1903, p. 453.

The total amount of revenue secured by the first settlement was Rs. 9,38,610 which showed an increase of Rs. 5,74,471 over the old jama of Rs. 3,64,139 as detailed below:-

TABLE – 5.3

Parguna	*Old jama*	*First settlement jama*	*Increase*
Mekhliganj	54,169	1,29,555	75,386
Mathabhanga	71,246	1,72,904	1,01,658
Lalbazar	74,476	1,34,198	59,722
Dinhata	76,451	1,74,034	97,583
Coochbehar	71,520	2,32,040	1,60,520
Tufanganj	16,277	95,879	79,602
Total =	3,64,139	9,38,610	5,74,471

Source: H.N.Chaudhury, *Cooch Behar State and its lands revenue settlement*, 1903, p.453.

The important feature of this settlement was that the state was not in possession of any informationof the undertenures of the jotes. These undertenures of which there were no less than six at the time. They were in order of successive lower grade: ***Jote, chukani, Dar chukani, Dar-a-dar chukani, Tasya chukani, Tali chukani*** and ***Tasya tali chukani***.[26] The profit of each upper stage in collecting the rent from the next lower stage was also recorded.

The settlement was concluded with the jotedars, varied from 8 to 13 years and ended in 1883–1884. His Highness was however pleased to extend it to 5 years, so His Highness sanctioned a general settlement of the state and operations had commenced from 1886–1887. In the meantime another petty settlement known as the ***Patit Charcha*** settlement had taken place between 1884 and 1886.[27] These settlement was taken in hand to assess the fallow lands which had come under cultivation since the first settlement. The Re-settlement of 1886 was known as the ***Rakam charcha*** settlement. The details of the classification of the lands and the fixation of rents were given bellow:-

TABLE – 5.4

Rates per Bighas

Class of Land	*1st Class*			*2nd Class*			*3rd Class*		
	Rs.	As.	P	Rs.	As.	P	Rs.	As.	P
Betelnut	4	0	0	4	0	0	4	0	0
Bastu	3	0	0	3	0	0	3	0	0
Udbastu	3	0	0	3	0	0	3	0	0
Garden	3	0	0	3	0	0	3	0	0
Bamboo	1	0	2	1	0	2	1	0	2
Tobacco 1st class	1	0	8	1	0	8	1	0	8
Tobacco 2nd class	1	0	4	1	0	4	1	0	4
Tobacco 3rd class	1	0	0	1	0	0	1	0	0
Awal	1	0	0	1	0	0	1	0	0
Diam	0	0	12	0	0	14	0	0	13
Saiam	0	0	9	0	0	11	0	0	10

Chaharam	0	0	7	0	0	8	0	0	7
San	0	0	7	0	0	6	0	0	5
Laik patit	0	0	2	0	0	6	0	0	5
Garlaik patit	0	0	1	0	0	2	0	0	2
Jala	0	8	8	0	0	1	0	0	1

Source: Durgadas Majumdar, *West Bengal District Gazetteers*, Koch Behar, 1977, p. 76.

In the course of the re-settlement operations, one of the chief features was the classification of the ***Taluks.*** O'Donnel was fixing the boundaries of Taluks. The numbers of Taluks given in Richard Ahmuty's register were 1099. The number ascertained'by O'Donnel Survey of *1202.*[28] The area under re-settlement was 21,23,696 ***Bighas*** comprising with 1,202 ***Taluks*** as shows below.

TABLE – 5.5

Name of Parganas, Taluks increased under Re-settlement

Name of Pargana	*Number of Taluks*	*Land under Re-settlement in bighas*
Mekhliganj	237	2,97,265
Matabhanga	189	3,82,172
Lalbabar	131	2,87,802
Dinhata	256	3,61,599
Cooch Behar	274	5,08,614
Tufanganj	115	2,86,244
Total =	1,202	21,23,696

Source: *Annual Administrative Report of Cooch Behar State*, 1886-87, p. 44.

It would appear that in the course of the two decades that intervened between the first settlement and re-settlement, there was an increase of 44,196 bighas in the assessed land. This increase was due to the settlement in jote right of 10,874 Bighas of resumed rent-free land and

33,322 Bighas of *khas* land.[29] The details are given below.

1.Assessed lands

		Bighas
Land recorded at the first Settlement =		21,65,620
Add.......		
Rent free lands resumed and Settled in jote right since the First settlement	10,874 =	44196
Khas lands settled in jote Right		33,322
Total =		**22,09816**
Deduct.........		
Rent free gants made out of assessed Lands since the First settlement		2389
Lands made khas or	83731 =	86,120
Bighas of decrease		
Re-dinguished...		
Difference.............		=21,23,696 Bighas

Being the quantity of land record At the re-settlement

II Rent free lands

Lands record at the first settlement Bighas.........85,389

Add.................	
Rent free grants made from assessed ...... Bighas of increase	2,389
Total=	87,778 Bighas
Deduct	
Lands resumed and settled in jote right —	10,874
Lands which become khas....................	840
Total	**=11,714 Bighas Decrease**
Differences	

Refresenting lands recorded at the..................76064 Bighas

Re-settlement.

III khas lands

Lands recorded at the first settlement.............1,68,869 Bighas

Add....

Lands made khas from assessed area	83,731
Do from rent free lands	840
New accretion 34556 =	1,19,127 Bighas of increase
Total=	2,87,996 Bighas

Deduct ....

Lands settled in jote right since the ....33,322 Bighas decrease

First settlement.

Difference representing lands records ....254,674 Bighas.[30]

The revenue before the re-settlement amounted Rs. 9,52,642 as noticed above. The re-settlement jama was Rs. 12,41,060. The increase obtained by this revision of the settlement therefore amounted to Rs. 288418 or 30 percent of the former revenue.[31] The details of the Re-assessment are given in Table 5.6.

It would be seen that the increase was not uniform everywhere or in every mehal. In Mathabhanga, Mekhliganj and Lalbazar the proportion of increase in the Debutter mehals exceeded that in the Mal Mahals, while in the remaining three parganas, the case was exactly the reverse. The Debutter jotes in the first three parganas were situated in rich tracts, and thus fetched better jamas than the average Mal jote. In the remaining three parganas the ***Mal Mehals*** possessed better soil than the Debutter mehals. This fact

Table 5.6

Name of pargana	*First settlement jama including patit increase*			*Re-settlement Jama*			*Increase at re-settlement*			*Percentage*		
	Mal	*Debutter*	*Total*	*Mal*	*Debutter*	*Total*	*Mal*	*Debutter*	*Total*	*Mal*	*Debutter*	*Total*
	Rs.	*Rs.*	*Rs.*	*Rs.*	*Rs.*	*Rs.*	*Rs.*	*Rs.*	*Rs.*	*Rs.*	*Rs.*	*Rs.*
Mekhliganj	127943	5985	133928	167486	7984	175470	39543	1999	41542	30	33	31
Mathabhanga	165523	15010	180533	218278	20701	238979	52755	5691	58446	31	37	32
Lalbazar	137964	3142	141106	176808	4368	181176	38844	1226	40070	28	37	29
Dinhata	167771	10081	177852	225877	12928	238805	58106	2847	60953	34	37	34
Coochbehar	191391	34776	226167	240864	41692	282556	49473	6916	56389	25	19	24
Tufanganj	76296	16760	93056	103460	20614	20614	124074	27164	3854	35	23	33
Total	866888	85754	952642	1132773	108287	1241060	265885	22533	288418	30	26	30

Source : Annual Administrative Report of Cooch Behar State, 1889 p. 32.

accounts for the inequality of the percentage of the increase in respect of these two mehals.[32] As for the total increase, it amounted to 31 percent in Mekhliganj, 32 percent is Mathabhanga, 29 percent in Lalbazar, 34 percent in Dinhata 24 percent in Cooch Behar, and 33 percent is Tufanganj. The largest percentage was thus attained in Dinhata and the smallest in Cooch Behar.

The amount of revenue charged on a jote, on an average was Rs. 56-7-6 at the first settlement; it came up to Rs. 65-14-1 at the re-settlement, showing an increase of 9-6-7. The details for the different parganas are given below -

TABLE – 5.7

Name of Parganas	*The average of First settlement*			*Resettlement*			*Variation*		
	Rs.	As.	P	Rs.	As.	P	Rs.	As.	P
Mekhliganj	70	1	5	75	9	7	5	8	2
Matabhanga	75	6	8	94	7	9	19	1	1
Lalbabar	53	6	6	69	9	1	16	2	7
Dinhata	46	9	5	60	0	0	13	6	7
Cooch Behar	46	2	6	52	15	1	6	12	7
Tufanganj	78	10	5	60	1	3	18	9	2
Total	56-	7-	6	65-	14-	1	9	6	7

Source: H.N.Chaudhury, *Cooch Behar State and Its Lands Revenue Settlement*, 1903, p. 475.

As could be expected, the jama of a jote rose everywhere except Tufanganj, where it came down from Rs. 78-10-05 to Rs. 60-01-03; marking a decrease of Rs.18-09-02. Although the average area of jote fell off in every pargana at the later settlement the decrease in Tufanganj was the highest, having come down from 237 Bighas to 138 Bighas. This fact accounted for the decrease of the *jama* in this pargana. The highest average jama now fetched by a jote was Rs. 94-7-9 in Mathabhanga; and the smallest Rs. 53 in Cooch Behar.[33]

The re-settlement fixed the revenue rates at which the

jotedars were to pay the revenue to the state. In the first settlement the rate of rent to be paid by the under tenure was not fixed. All that was done was to fix the rate of the jotedars and to provide that each class of superior interest so as to get 25 percent as profit.

The Re-settlement observed the following scale -

1. Percentage in case in which the **Dara-dar choukanidar** was the last under tenant in the scale-

	Rs.
Jotedar............................	35
Chukanidar....................	15
Darchukanidar..................	10

2. Percentages in cases where the **Tasya chukanidar** was the last under tenant in the scale

	Rs.
Jotedar..............................	35
Chukanidar...................	10
Darchukanidar.................	10
Dare-dar Chukanidar.........................	5

3. Percentage in case in which the **Tali Chukamindar** was the last under tenant in the scale -

	Rs.
Jotedar..........................	35
Chukanidar...................	10
Darchukanidar.................	5
Dare-dar Chukanidar...........	5
Tasya chukamidar...............	5

4. Percentages in case in where the Tasya Tali was the under tenant

	Rs.
Jotedar...........................	35
Chukanidar....................	5
Darchukanidar.................	5
Dare-dar Chukanidar	5
Tasya chukanidar...............	5
Tali chukanidar.................	5

Source: Durgadas Majumdar, *West Bengal District Gazetteer*, Koch Behar, 1977, p. 147.

The fixed profit was allowed to the jotedar in the above scheme to ensure security of the revenue of the state and to keep the jotes attractive, for it was the jotedar who had to pay the revenue under paid in case of default.

The *Rakam charcha* re-settlement was to expire in about 1918 - 1920. As there had been but only one survey of the state in 1868 – 70, it was decided to have another complete survey before the next Re-settlement. Accordingly, a traverse survey and a cadastral survey was undertaken from 1912 and ended in 1916 – 1917. The expiring settlements of the *Rakam charcha* settlement were extended and in 1927 a new Re-settlement was made on the basis of the new survey. The total revenue demand secured by the 1927 settlement was a little over Rs. 18 lakhs.[34] The settlement of 1913 – 1927 which was given effect to from 1927 – 1928 were about to expire in 1956 when the Estates Acquisition Act was enforced in Cooch Behar. The towns and bunders were under settlement in 1943 – 1944 and as this settlement were for a period of ten years these also expired about this time.

5.2 Stamp Revenue

At the time of Maharaja Narendra Narayan stamp paper was introduced in the Cooch Behar Courts. Before Maharaja Narendra Narayan there was not use stamp paper in the courts of Cooch Behar State. The stamp was in vogue a system of charging fees on cases instituted was called the name of "institution fees".[35] The introduction of stamps was a reform effected by the late Mharaja who passed a stamp Act on the 25th *Magh* 1268 B.E. corresponding with 1865. When the Act was passed, there was Superintendent of stamp but after that the office of the Superintendent of stamp was abolished and in place of that the sale of stamps was made over to the Deputy Muktear.[36] In 1865, H.G. Beveridge, Deputy Commissioner of Cooch Behar state, transferred the charge of the office to the Officer in charge of the ***Nikasi Adalat*** or the Account office. In 1868, the post of the superintendent of stamp was revived but later again abolished on the November, 1872.[37] The office was transferred to Treasury office and the charge of the Treasury was under Dewan of the state of Cooch Behar.

The Cooch Behar state firstly used the "Imressed stamps". For the first time but latter, in 1872, there were only two kinds of stamp papers in use, namely General stamps and peon-fee or court-fee stamps. All these stamps had circular red impressions.[38]

The Commissioner of Cooch Behar State sanctioned the manufacture of documentary stamps with blue impression on 1876, therefore, three different kinds of stamps came to use in the State, namely, Judicial, Documentary and Court fee. In 1884 – 1885, copying-fee stamps with green impressions were introduced. The use of ordinary paper suitors in the courts of the state was stopped and Pice-cartridge paper was introduced for taking its place in 1890–1891.[39]

In 1872 Colonel Haughton indented stamp papers from England and a supply of Stamps was received from that country in December of that year. The value of papers was high and demand was not fulfilled. So, these stamps were then produced in Cooch Behar and there was a ***chheptakar*** or printer attached to the stamp office. The stamps began to be printed by the state press after its transfer to Cooch Behar under the supervision of the treasury Officer.[40] The Treasury officer the ex-officio superintendent of stamps supervised the manufacturing of stamps. The Cooch Bhear

Treasury was the central stamp depot, from which stamps were issued to the Sub-Treasuries.

The stamps revenue of the state was a history of rapid progress for other source of income. In 1864 – 1865 the stamp revenue amounted to Rs. 25965, and year 1883 – 1884 was 1,32,833 and it came upto Rs.170730 in 1899 – 1900.[41]

The stamp revenue was controlled by two administrations, the British administration and the direct administration under His Highness. The stamps Revenue of Cooch Behar State is given below-

TABLE – 5.8

Details of Stamps Revenue of Cooch Behar States (1864 – 1900)

Years	*Judicial*	*Documentary*	*Court-fee*	*Other description*	*Total*
1864-65	25965	-	-	-	25965
1865-66	32717	-	-	-	32717
1866-67	53648	-	-	-	53648
1867-68	63339	-	-	-	6339
1868-69	69433	-	-	-	69433
1869-70	71226	-	-	-	71226
1870-71	76503	-	-	-	76503
1871-72	77639	-	-	-	87315
1872-73	72622	-	15454	-	88076
1873-74	71247	-	19792	-	91039
1874-75	79512	-	25172	-	104684
1875-76	75746	-	21073	-	96819
1876-77	69657	24327	25613	-	119603
1877-78	66789	24139	25853	-	116781
1878-79	82019	25826	32377	-	140252
1879-80	128251	92532	44355	-	205138
1880-81	61942	20395	31739	-	114076
1881-82	67501	24897	31739	-	123796
1882-83	68834	27501	31622	-	127957
1883-84	72371	26312	33550	-	132838
1884-85	85092	26812	37710	885	150499

1885-86	84534	26298	41055	2086	153973
1886-87	83526	23427	4074	2013	149670
1887-88	79312	23765	38413	2306	143796
1888-89	80694	22331	39927	2401	145353
1889-90	78950	20515	36896	2389	138750
1890-91	75583	21860	31585	2441	131469
1891-92	83075	25881	34605	2865	146426
1892-93	92172	27284	36120	3243	158819
1893-94	89486	25933	34738	3249	153406
1894-95	94324	26898	36157	4063	161442
1895-96	84665	36669	33477	5340	160151
1896-97	94397	37183	35939	3612	171131
1897-98	103437	29069	38776	4233	175515
1898-99	117712	32902	36587	4485	192686
1899-1900	103404	29730	32656	3940	170730

Source: Durgadas Majumder, *West Bengal District Gazetteers*, Koch Behar, 1977, pp. 153-154.

TABLE – 5. 9

Details of Stamp Revenue from (1910 – 1941)

Years	*Total stamp revenue*
1910-11	200700
120-21	253600
1930-31	275200
1940-41	285300

Source: *Annual Administrative Report of Cooch Behar State* for the relevant years.

5.3 Revenue from the Forest Products

The forest was naturally one of the most important sources of revenue of the state. In Cooch Behar State, this department was established in 1882–1883 and it was under the supervision of kumar Gajendra Narayan (Jr.). But after that, such forests as the state possessed had hitherto been under the charge of the Superintendent of the public works Department. The authority had given their attention to increase the area under forests for future generations and several young nurseries had been planted out. There were several experimental teak plantations in different parts of the state including the two sub-divisional towns of Mathabhanga and Mekhliganj, which were about 12 years old at the date of opening of the department and required preservation and looking the forests.[42] The department mainly emphasized the plantation of timber and shady trees in different parts of the state. The existing sal, Teak and shishu forests were taken care of and measure were adopted to extend sal and shishu plantations.

Between the year 1884–1885 and 1892–93, twenty one plantations of shishu trees, covering an area of about 2000 Bighas were done.[43] A table is given below showing the number of plantations in 1892–93.

Name of place	Numbers of Plantation
Chegirghat	4
Balasi Nababganj	1
Suktabari	1
Baraibari	2
Charakerkuthi	3
Nilkuthi	2
Khagrabari	1
Haldibari	4
Balasi Natuarpar	1
Hadumdanga	1
Kholta	1
Total =	**21**

The net outlay on the forests and plantations from 1882–83 to 1892–93 was about Rs. 11,000

5.4 Excise Revenue

Excise Revenue was the important sub-head of the revenue

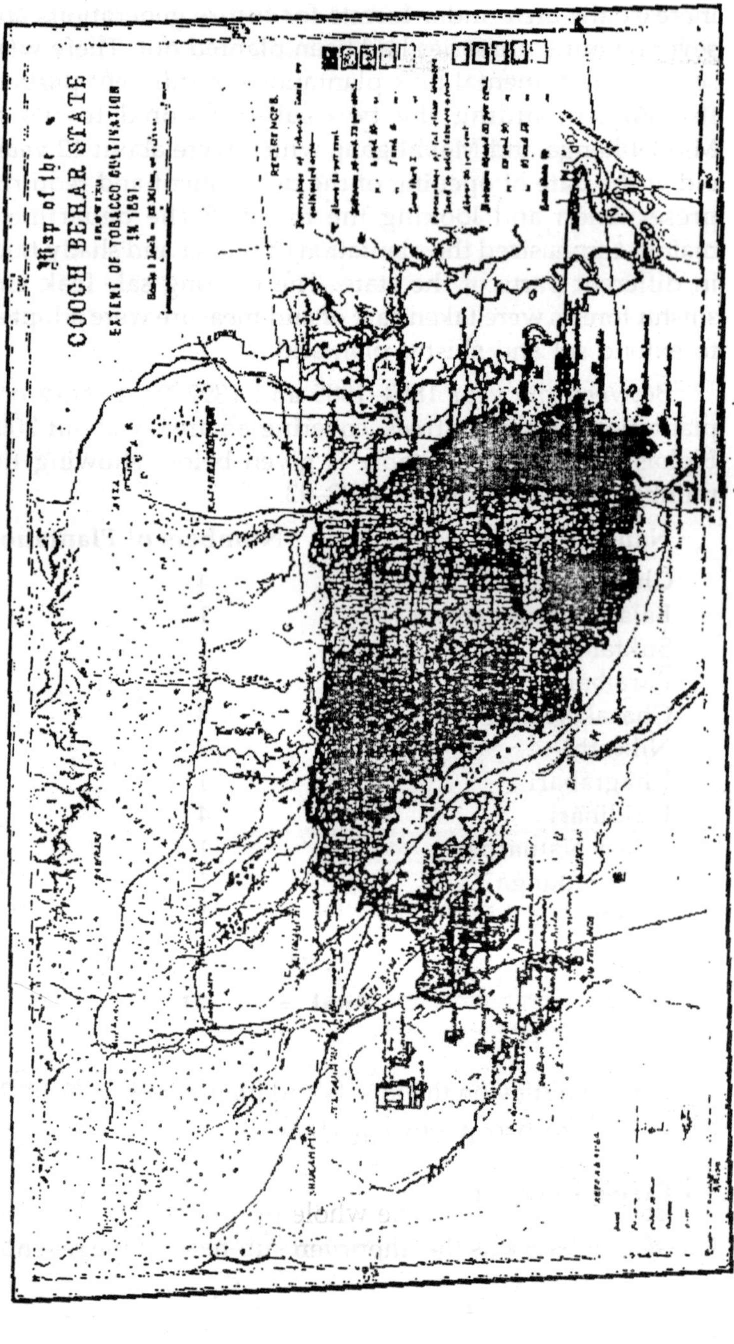
Map of the
COOCH BEHAR STATE
SHOWING
EXTENT OF TOBACCO CULTIVATION
IN 1891.
REFERENCES.

of the Cooch Behar State. Formerly the excise revenue came from two sources-***Abkari Mehals*** and ***Mushkarat Mehals.*** The Abkari Mehals included all rights connected with the manufacture and sale of State spirits. On the other hand, the Mushkarat mehals had reference to the sale of *opium* and *ganja*. These mehals used to be a price at an auction by the Dewan to the highest bidder. The purchaser of the *Abkari* Mehals enjoyed a monopoly for the whole State and he could open shops wherever he pleased. For this situation the revenue derived from auction sale was very small amounted to Rs. 86 only in 1864.[44] The farmer could sell their liquor cheaply and the number of drug shops increased and also drinking habit among the people was increased in Cooch Behar State. H. Beveridge, the Deputy Commissioner of Cooch Behar State noticing in 1864–65 the complaints were common that drunkuness was daily on a increase.[45]

The poppy was used to the growth of opium manufacturing the State under former Maharaja. Before 1867, no positive step was taken against the cultivation. When Colonel Haughton came to Cooch Behar as Commissioner, he prohibited the cultivation of poppy in Cooch Behar under specified penalties, on the Government agreeing to supply the drug to the State at cost price, which was fixed at Rs. 7–4 per ***seer***[46] and State realized a duty at Rs. 22 a ***seer***.[47]

In the case of ***Ganja***, the farmer formerly made his own arrangements for procuring the drug from Rangpur, the Government realizing the duty on the quantity purchased by him. On representation being made to Government that the Maharaja was entiled to levy duty on the Ganja consumed with in his own territory, authority was given in the middle of 1871 to procure Ganja at cost price from Rajshahi.[48] The State had since got its own goladars as in the Government districts. Later a very inferior sort of ***ganja*** was also grown by the people near their houses; this practice was stopped long ago. The whole of the duty in the case of both opium and ***ganja*** then went to the State as revenue, no royalty being charged by Government on what they sell to the State.

The Government excise system was introduced into the State and an ***Abkari Daroga*** was appointed under the Dewan as officer being selected.[49] Under Dewan, the excise department was fully organized, and its revenue had been continued to expand steadily upto the second half of Nineteenth Century. On September, 1869 State Distillery system was opened at Cooch Behar and Mekhliganj.

5.5 Other Sources of Revenue

Among other sources of revenue of the State was a large number of petty taxes-

a) Tobacco, Jute and Mustard seeds

These were the main commercial crops produced in the Cooch Behar State.Both of these were grown in abundance in the land cultivation. The collection of revenue from exportation of Tobacco, Jute and Mustard seeds were made through farmers. According to Mercer and Chauvet Report in 1788, the main export goods were Tobacco-40, 000 maunds, Mustard seeds-10, 000 maunds, Jute-20,000 mauds.In 1872, W.W.Hunnter in his statistical Account of Cooch Behar had given details that the chief export goods from the State were tobacco, jute and mustard seeds .According to him, the Native Merchants estimated the exports at $150,000 per annum.The export trade of Cooch Behar State has been given below-

TABLE – 5.10: Name of Articles and Their Values

Name of Article	*Amount(mds)*	*Values (Rs)*
Tobacco	400000	200000
Jute	300000	120000
Mustard seeds	25000	10000
Total	7,25000	33,00000

Source: H.N.Chaudhury, *Cooch Behar State and its Land Revenue Settlement*, 1903, p. 194.

TABLE – 5.11

The year-wise list of export goods from Cooch Behar State has been given below (1900-1950)

Years	*Tobacco (mds)*	*Jute (mds)*	*Mustard seeds (mds)*
1900-1901	482300	270797	24000
1910-1911	548211	385050	30000
1920-1921	540247	462500	48005
1930-1931	691701	496000	52000
1940-1941	731250	510213	84000
1950	830254	769705	100200

Source: *Annual Administration Report of the Cooch Behar State* for the relevant Years.

B) Bunders:

Cooch Behar State Agencies collected money from the local Merchants and foreign Merchants as a toll tax from different Bunders or Hàts. The collection of revenue is given below-

TABLE – 5.12

The Year-wise collection of Toll taxes from Cooch Behar State have been given below (1900-1951)

Years	*Collection as a Toll taxes (Rs)*
1900-1901	921
1910-1911	1102
1920-1921	798
1930-1931	1201
1940-1941	1278
1950-1951	1560

Source: *Annual Administrative Report of Cooch Behar State for the relevant Years.*

C) Fairs

The annual fairs were held as usual at Dinhata, Haldibari, Cooch Behar, Mekhliganj, Fulbari and collection of fees was made over to the respective Town Committees. Besides this big fair, there was also small type of fairs held on different parts of the State. The fairs continued to attract a large number of shopkeepers, and the sales were brisk as usual. The details are given below-

TABLE – 5.13: Fairs and Collection of Taxes

Years	*Fairs*	*Revenue Collection (Rs)*
1900-1901	Rashjatra, Janmastami, Snan mela, Sib Ratri.	1802
1910-1911		1556
1920-1921		1920
1930-1931		2090
1940-1941		2011
1950		2310

Source: *Annual Administrative Report of Cooch Behar State for the relevant Years.*

D) Khas Mahel

The Department was under the control of the Revenue Minister of the State throughout the year. The annual revenue of Rs.6663 was made over to the khas Mahel Department during the year.

E) Railways

Before 1876, there was no Railway within Cooch Behar State. In 1876, North Bengal Railway opened a station at Haldibari in Cooch Behar State.[50] This line later became the main line of the Eastern Bengal Railway connecting Calcutta with Siliguri and Darjeeling. After that, Maharaja of Cooch Behar constructed a Railway line from Mogalhat to Cooch Behar in 1894. In 1901, the Railway was working from Gitaldaha to Alipurduar, establishing a link with the Assam link portion of North East Frontier Railway, while the Bamanhat-Gitaldaha section was working as a branch line. The Cooch Behar State Railway was in profitable position. The table is shown the Revenue from Railway (1900 – 1950) -

TABLE – 5.14

Revenue from Railway (1900-1950) has been given below

Years	*Revenue collection (Rs)*	*Expenditure (Rs)*	*Increase (Rs)*
1900-1901	97146	50,000	47146
1910-1911	217388	115020	102368
1920-1921	319424	146802	172622
1930-1931	376828	174410	202418
1940-1941	434202	197120	237082
1950	512155	200166	311989

Source: *Annual Administrative Report of Cooch Behar State for the relevant Years.*

NOTES AND REFERENCES

1. Biswanath Das and Subhendu Majumder, *Princely Cooch Behar: A documentary study on letters (1790–1863 AD)*, p. 7.
2. *Cooch Behar Select Records*, Vol. I, 1882, p. 232.
3. *Ibid*, p. 457.
4. H. N. Chaudhury, *Cooch Behar State and its Land Revenue Settlement*, Cooch Behar, 1903, p. 453.
5. *Loc.cit.*
6. *Loc.cit.*
7. *Loc.cit.*
8. *Loc.cit.*
9. W.W. Hunter, *A Statistical Account of Bengal*, Vol. X, pp. 428-30.
10. *Ibid*, p. 582.
11. Todormal, *op. cit.*, p. 73.

12. H. N.Chaudhury, *op.cit.*, p. 569.
13. Henry Douglas Report to the Governor General, *Cooch Behar Select Records*, Vol. I, p. 45.
14. *Ibid.*, pp. 29-34.
15. H. N. Chaudhury, *op.cit.*, pp. 444-445.
16. Durgadas Majumder, *West Bengal District Gazetteers*, Koch Behar, 1977, p. 147.
17. Captain F. Jenkins, *Diary and Notes*, Calcutta, 1868, p. 20.
18. Proceedings of Revenue Department, July, 1872, No–210.
19. Proceedings of Revenue Department, August, 1872, No 210.
20. *Loc. cit.*
21. *Loc. cit.*
22. H. N. Chaudhury, *op.cit.*, p. 459.
23. *Ibid*, p. 457.
24. Cooch Behar Gazette, p. 144.
25. *Ibid*, p. 145.
26. *Ibid*, p. 146.
27. Annual Administrative Report of Cooch Behar State, 1884 – 85, p. 7.
28. H. N. Chaudhury, *op.cit.*, p. 466.
29. *Ibid*, p.467.
30. Annual Administrative Report of Cooch Behar State, 1889, p. 32.
31. H. N. Chaudhury, *op.cit.*, p. 468.
32. *Ibid*, p.580.
33. *Ibid*, p.582.
34. Durgadas Majumder, *op.cit.*, p. 149.
35. H. N. Chaudhury, *op.cit.*, p. 375.
36. *Ibid*, p. 376.

37. Annual Administrative Report of Cooch Behar State, 1877, p. 38.
38. Proceedings of Revenue Department, July, 1872, No. 210.
39. Annual Administrative Report of Cooch Behar state, 1890 –91, p. 22.
40. Proceedings of Revenue Dept. July, 1872, No. 210.
41. H. N. Chaudhury, *op.cit.*, pp. 375–76.
42. *Ibid*, p. 395.
43. *Ibid*, p. 582.
44. *Ibid*, p. 584.
45. *Ibid*, p.586.
46. Para II of the Resolution of the Government of Bengal, Dated 17th September 1866, on the Administrative Report of Cooch Behar for 1865–66.
47. *Annual Administrative Report of Cooch Behar State*, 1865 – 66, Excise Department, para- 4.
48. *Ibid*, p.582.
49. H. N. Chaudhury, *op.cit.*, p. 374.
50. Durgadas Majumder, *op.cit.*, p. 119.

APPENDIX - 5.A: Heading of information relative to the re-assessment of the State.

1	2	3	4	5	6	7	8	9	10	11	12	13
		Unassessed land					Assessed Land.					
Name of Pargana	Extent in Bighas	Patit land, jungle, Churs, swamps, &c.	Hats, roads, &c. and lands incapable of cultivation	Service	Rent-free	Total	Cultivated	Culturable	Total	First settlement jama	Jama on the eve of re-settlement	Re-settlement jama
	B K D	B K D	B K D	B K D	B K D	B K D	B K D	B K D	B K D	RS AS P	RS AS P	RS AS P
Mekhliganj	372417 2 7	5034 3 7	27251 8 19	...	[illegible]	33597 3 15	254142 4 11	74677 13 18	308819 15 9	175665 [illegible]	138500 11 3	130042 3 10
Mathabhanga	428286 4 7	4551 13 9	24675 9 4	2,930 [illegible]	7313 5 9	5679 1 9	287990 11 4	101898 15 17	389689 3 1	175900 3 3	183764 10 [illegible]	240208 9 2
Lalbazar	333229 1 13	2973 6 0	25754 9 3	882 11 1	15115 10 5	64736 9 9	234522 3 10	53877 2 14	288493 3 4	134198 5 11	141249 5 7	151319 11 9
Dinhata	409982 12 11	6785 13 5	25253 5 3	140 13 2	8256 15 13	41662 5 4	257086 14 19	67333 9 14	364330 4 [illegible]	174033 10 4	178548 8 6	239501 1 [illegible]
Cooch Behar	602133 12 12	17973 [illegible]	155575 11 2	13554 4	[illegible]	58451 [illegible]	368790 [illegible]	145999 17 7	813679 13 [illegible]	[illegible]	226[illegible] 2 5	296[illegible] 3 [illegible]
Tufanganj	389082 14 5	33668 12 19	42813 19 4	1390 4 [illegible]	4344 [illegible]	[illegible]	192547 3 17	93516 2 11	286362 6 4	[illegible]	53056 12 6	129104 2 5
Total	2512133 5 2	68037 9 0	169535 5 14	19177 1 [illegible]	[illegible]	[illegible] 12 11	1542379 2 15	538996 12 16	2181375 15 3	[illegible] 2	359830 5 [illegible]	[illegible] 5 2

Source: H.N. Choudhary, the Cooch Behar State and its Land Revenue Settlement, 1903, p. 615.

APPENDIX - 5.B

Headings of information relative to the re assessment of PARGANA MEKHLIGANJ

1	2	3	4	5	6	7	8	9	10	11	12	13	14
			Unassessed land					Assessed Land					
Name of Pargana	Name of Mehal	Extent of Taluk	Buildings, paths, tanks, swamps &c.	Riverbed, road & distances incapable of cultivation	Service	Rent-free	Total	Cultivated	Culturable	Total	First settlement Jama	Jama of the eve of re-settlement	Re-settlement jama
		B K D	B K D	B K D	B K D	B K D	B K D	B K D	B K D	B K D	Rs As p	Rs. As P	Rs. As P
Mekhliganj	Mal Jote	165082 5 6	2023 16 [illegible]	13993 15 5	..	4452 [illegible] 4	20474 12 6	113416 7 16	34191 9 4	144607 17 0	86366 1 0	68531 4 5	87696 1 9
	Debottar Jotes	13206 4 [illegible]	[illegible]	7038 5 14			[illegible] 6 2	9641 2 13	2393 15 5	12034 17 18	3569 7 9	5885 9 8	7984 4 5
	Mokarari Mehal	1075 4 4	721 16 [illegible]				721 16 0	34714 2 8	5635 3 16	40353 6 4	4441 0 0	4441 0 0	4441 0 0
	Total	219363 12 11	[illegible]	[illegible] 4 19		4457 16 4	[illegible] 16 9	157772 12 17	39274 4 5	196996 1 2	74368 8 8	79357 14 5	100320 6 2
Rahimganj	Mal Jotes	56921 7 13	[illegible]	5217 16 17		454 [illegible] 9	[illegible] 17 7	[illegible] 8 0	21554 2 12	89716 10 13	38063 11 6	37654 7 8	57794 11 2
	Mokarari Mehal	1204 5 11		[illegible] 2 4			[illegible] 0 4	800 12 5	4[illegible] 9 2	120[illegible] 2 7	[illegible] 4 9	13[illegible] 0 5	131 9 9
	Total	58125 13 4	[illegible]	5216 2 [illegible]		454 [illegible] 9	[illegible] 0 5	[illegible] 1 5	22284 11 14	90417 12 19	38195 9 3	37786 1 3	52826 4 11
Kote Bhajni Jeldhar	Mal Jotes	22547 14 8	[illegible]	117 4 19		194 [illegible]	[illegible] 6 19	17033 10 16	4775 16 11	21809 7 9	5079 17 8	9307 1 2	12361 5 0
	Mal Jotes	37464 17 6	327 [illegible]	2465 16 19			[illegible] 5	21203 15 11	8392 17 6	29596 16 19	11911 3 10	12049 10 9	14434 3 9
	Grand Total	372417 2 7	5014 [illegible]	22551 8 18		5011 11 13	33495 3 18	264142 4 11	74677 13 14	338818 18 8	129555 2 7	138500 11 3	108042 3 10

Source: Do, p. 616.

APPENDIX - 5.C: Headings of information relative to the re-assessment of PARGANA MATHABHANGA ANDLAL BAZAR

1	2	3	4	5	6	7	8	9	10	11	12	13	14
			Unassessed land					Assessed Land.					
Name of Pargana	Name of Mehal	Extent in Bighas	Patit land, jungle, churs swamps & c	Hats, roads & c, and lands incapable of cultivation	Service	Rent-free	Total	Cultivated	Cultivable	Total	First settlement Jama	Jama on the eve of re-settlement	Re-settlement jama
		B K D	B K D	B K D	B K D	B K D	B K D	B K D	B K D	B K D	RS As P	Rs As P	RS. As P
Mathabhanga	[illegible]	381144 2 9	4506 0 5	22429 14 5	2932 10 10	7132 0 9	3130 5 5	[illegible]	20562 13 6	344145 17 0	156 [illegible]	153234 1 6	215151 0 5
	Debottar Jotes	34599 16 16	132 7 4	2210 7 8			2342 14 [illegible]	[illegible]	[illegible] 15 5	[illegible]	[illegible] 6 8	15010 4 6	20700 7 4
	Mokarari Mehal	7523 17 1	4 12 0	1 18 17			6 10 17	[illegible] 3 4	[illegible] 1 0	7517 6 4	1230 15 10	1230 15 10	1230 15 10
	Total	423267 18 6	4602 19 8	24642 0 14	2932 10 10	7132 0 9	39349 10 17	[illegible]	[illegible] 15 14	383913 5 9	[illegible] 9 4	179475 5 10	237087 [illegible]
Bashkatar chhit	Mal Jotes	2993 18 10	8 14 1	23 4 5	..	387 7 14	219 8 0	2756 [illegible]	429 9 0	2774 10 10	1321 1 5	1373 10 11	1773 2 11
Maraghat baishchala	Mal Jotes	3006 11 11	..	10 4 8			10 4 9	[illegible]	[illegible] 3	2996 7 2	531 45 6	915 9 6	1353 14 [illegible]
	Total	429268 4 7	4864 13 9	24675 9 4	2932 10 10	7519 5 1	39579 1 6	[illegible]	[illegible] 11 17	[illegible] 3 1	[illegible] 3	181764 10 1	240209 9 2
	PARGANA LALBAZAR												
	Mal Jotes	326344 12 0	2948 19 8	25410 8 18	892 [illegible]	[illegible] 6	[illegible] 11 12	[illegible]	[illegible] 2 16	281967 0 8	[illegible] 2 4	137963 14 19	178807 15 5
	Debottar Mehal	6193 4 15	14 8 12	344 0 5			358 5 17	[illegible] 1	[illegible] 15 14	5534 17 14	2328 11 1	3141 11 6	4368 3 0
Kote bhajani	Mokarari Mehal (Mal)	600 3 10		...				[illegible]	[illegible] 0	[illegible] 6 [illegible]	[illegible] 4	[illegible]35 4 [illegible]	175 4 [illegible]
leldhar	Mokarari Mehal (Debottar)	90 19 5		..				90 [illegible]	[illegible] 15 4	90 13 5	3 5 3	8 5 3	5 5 3
	Total	333297 1 13	2973 6 0	25754 9 3	892 13 0	15115 [illegible]	44435 18 3	234522 [illegible]	[illegible] 2 14	288493 3 4	144188 0 1	141249 5 7	181319 [illegible]

Source: Do, p. 617.

APPENDIX - 5.D: Headings of information relative to the re-assessment of PARGANA MATHABHANGA ANDLAL BAZAR

1	2	3	4	5	6	7	8	9	10	11	12	13	14
			Unassessed land					Assessed Land.					
Name of Pargana	Name of Mehal	Extent to Highest	Patit land, jungle, churs, swamps &c	Hats, roads & c, wns lands incapable of cultivation	Service	Rent-free	Total	Cultivated	Culturable	Total	First settlement Jama	Jama on the eve of re-settlement	Re-settlement jama
		B K D	B K D	B K D	B K D	B K D	B K D	B K D	B K D	B K D	RS As P	Rs As P	RS As P
Dinhata	Mal Jote	360778 10 15	6706 6 8	24576 19 2	342 13 2	6256 14 13	29886 14 5	278774 14 2	62177 2 8	340892 16 10	163768 15 8	167770 12 1	2258761? 6
	Debottar Jote	22422 15 5	40 10 6	1674 8 5			1716 18 11	15959 17 9	4742 19 5	20707 16 14	9565 10 2	10081 9 11	12928 1 4
	Mokuran Mehal	[illegible] 6 17	38 16 17	11 18 16			50 15 8	2362 3 8	368 8 1	2730 11 8	896 7 5	896 2 6	896 7 6
Bash-katar-chhit	Total	409482 12 17	6784 13 6	26263 8 3	342 13 2	6256 15 13	41657 6 4	297096 14 15	67233 9 14	364330 4 13	174033 12 4	178548 8 6	2395[illegible]
	PARGANA COOCH BEHAR												
Mara ghat	Mal Jotes	520539 6 7	1189312 19	42286 5 16	13504 10 2	16398 14 13	84083 [illegible] 10	305286 10 7	131186 8 9	436455 18 16	191450 3 5	191390 5 3	2436314 1
baish	Debottar Mehal	76526 11 1	8030 7 0	3288 15 8	45 10 2		4368 16 8	56563 15 8	15694 3 5	72157 14 15	32460 2 10	34778 2 8	41661 14 6
chala	Total	597061 16 1	1297319 18	45575 5 2	13564 0 4	16398 14 13	88452 4 18	361850 1 [illegible]	146783 13 14	508613 13 8	223910 6 3	226186 8 0	2825551 7
Kotel	Mokuran Mehal (Aial)	4471 17 4		1 8 0			. 5 0	3361 3 15	1109 5 5	4470 8 4	517 13 4	512 13 4	517 13 4
Bhajni Tengnai	Mokuran Mehal (Debottar)	586 17 1			...			509 1 18	29 16 3	586 17 1	31 14 2	31 14 2	31 14 2
	Total	602133 17 12	1290318 19	45576 16 2	13558 0 4	16398 14 13	85452 12 18	365780 7 12	147898 12 2	613678 19 14	274465 1 9	226711 3 9	283100 8 1

Source: Do, p. 618.

APPENDIX - 5.E: Headings of information relative to the re-assessment of PARGANA MATHABHANGA ANDLAL BAZAR

1	2	3	4	5	5	7	8	9	10	11	12	13	14
			Unassessed Land					Assessed Land					
Name of Pargana	Name of Mehal	Extent in Bighas	Patit land, jungle, churs, swamps & c.	Hats, roads & c. and lands incapable of cultivation	Service	Rent free	Total	Cultivated	Culturable	Total	First settlement Jama	Jama on the eve of re-settlement	Re-settlement Jama
		B. K. D.	B. K. D.	B. K. D.	B. K. D.	B. K. D.	B. K. D.	B. K. D.	B. K. D.	B. K. D.	Rs. As. P.	Rs. As. P.	Rs. As. P.
Tufanganj	Mal Jote	321785 6 1	3252010 0	40153 6 17	1390 4 [illegible]	4346 [illegible] 13	7910 17 12	159868 6 [illegible]	13006 7 2	242874 11 9	78415 12 9	75295 [illegible] 7	110469 3 6
	Detected Jotes	47178 9 12	1148 2 19	2000 12 7			5808 15 5	32859 18 [illegible]	10575 15 9	43369 14 6	17061 14 2	16760 0 [illegible]	20613 15 3
	Total	35[illegible] 15 13	3366812 19	42813 19 4	1390 4 17	4346 [illegible]	82719 7 16	192728 5 4	[illegible] 2 [illegible]	286244 7 15	95[illegible] 13 11	93055 13 [illegible]	124074 2 9
	Mokarari Mehal	118 18 13		...				118 18 13		118 18 13			30 0 0
	Total	309082 14 8	3366812 19	42813 19 4	1390 4 17	4846 [illegible] 13	82719 7 18	192847 3 11	13516 2 11	286363 6 8	95[illegible]8 10 11	93055 12 6	124104 2 9

Source: Do, p. 619.

APPENDIX - 5.F: Headings of information relative to the re-assessment of PARGANA TUFANGANJ

1	2	3	4	5	6	7	8	9	10	11	12	13	14
			Unassessed land					Assessed Land					
Name of Pargana	[illegible]	Extent in Bighas	Path land jungle, churs swamps & c	Hats, roads & c. and lands incapable of cultivation	Service	Rent free	Total	Cultivated	Culturable	Total	First settlement Jama	Jama on the eve of re-settlement	Re-settlement jama
		B K D	B K D	B K D	B K D	B K D	B K D	B K D	B K D	B K D	Rs As P	Rs As P	Rs As P
Tufanganj	Mal [illegible]	321785 6 1	3252010 0	40153 6 [illegible]	1390 4 17	4546 10 18	78910 12 12	156866 6 7	63006 7 2	242874 13 9	78816 12 8	76296 11 7	103469 3 6
	[illegible] lands	47178 8 12	1148 2 19	2560 12 7			4808 15 6	32659 12 17	12509 15 9	43365 14 6	17061 14 2	16760 0 11	20613 15 3
	Total	368963 15 13	3366… 2 19	42813 19 [illegible]	1390 4 17	4846 10 13	62719 7 18	192728 5 4	93516 2 1	286244 7 15	95878 10 11	93055 12 6	12408… 2 9
	[illegible] Mehal	118 18 13		....	....		....	118 18 15	....	118 18 13	....	....	38 0 [illegible]
	Total	369082 14 6	33660 2 19	42813 15 4	1390 4 17	4846 10 18	62719 7 19	192847 3 17	93516 2 11	286363 6 8	95878 10 11	93055 12 6	124101 2 4

Source: Do, p. 620.

APPENDIX - 5.G: Statement showing the member of jotedars and under-tenants of different grades, as also the quantity of land separately held by them, concemed with the area under re-settlement

by them concerned with the area under re-settlement

1	2	3	4	5	6	7	8	9	10	11	12	13	14	15	16	17
			Quantity of land Directly Head by													
Name of Pargana	Name of Mehal	Total of assessed land	Jotes	Chukanis	Dar Chukanis	Daradar Chukanis	Tasya Chukanis	Tai Chukanis	Tasya-Tail Chukanis	Number of Jotes	Chukanis	Dar-Chukanis	Daradar chukanis	Tasya-Chukanis	Tail-Chukanis	Tasya-Tail-Chukanis
Mekhliganj		297256 9 18	89000 7 18	137991 5 18	54002 17 1	13231 11 5	[illegible] 17 5	67 3 17	7 6 8	2321	6291	2869	687	103	13	1
Mathabhanga		382171 16 17	70000 9 4	164393 18 5	[illegible] 10	33007 15 1	5476 16 1	918 10 13	148 14 3	2529	5800	5061	2700	412	73	6
Lalbazar	..	287808 18 6	73659 2 11	134349 0 17	65276 11 19	13064 8 1	1444 16 1	65 18 15	—	2804	5106	3146	724	71	8	0
Dinhata	—	361399 13 4	65651 9 4	150644 12 14	112027 18 9	31507 3 18	5777 18 14	537 6 5	12 4 0	3880	11717	12419	5140	1121	128	8
Cooch-behar	-	508613 13 9	155632 15 3	227895 19 19	99636 11 14	23022 4 8	2553 8 0	35 14 5	—	5337	10668	8806	1981	287	6	0
Tufanganj		286244 7 15	120940 0 10	115571 13 9	40447 8 19	8847 14 14	1232 10 3		—	3066	3937	2200	559	98	0	0
Lalbazar		2123696 19 9	[illegible] 4 10	921616 10 16	474812 1 13	[illegible]	[illegible] 6 12	1620 13 15	168 4 11	18836	43534	32654	11136	2098	228	2

Source: H.N. Choudhary, the Cooch Behar State and its land Revenue Settlement, p. 670.

APPENDIX - 5.H: Number of jotedars and undertenants and the land held by them MEKHILIGANJ

1	2	3	4	5	5	7	8	9	10	11	12	13	14	15	15	17
			Quantity of land Directly Head by													
Name of Pargana	Name of Mehal	Total of assessed land.	Jotes	Chukanis	Dar Chukanis	Daradar Chukanis	Tasya Chukanis	Tail Chukanis	Tasya-Tail Chukanis	Number of Jotes	Chukanis	Dar-Chukanis	Daradar chukanis	Tasya-Chukanis	Ta-Chukanis	Tasya-Tail-Chukanis
Mekhliganj	[illegible]	144607 6 19	43044 6 16	61011 8 2	23775 [illegible]	[illegible]	1590 14 16	13 12 4	—	593	2514	1308	404	61	4	
Ditto	[illegible]	12034 17 19	1054 2 13	4771 6 4	[illegible]	[illegible]	370 11 4	11 3 14	7 6 8	32	154	161	91	6	6	7
Total		156642 14 19	44098 14 4	65782 14 6	[illegible]	[illegible]	1970 5 0	[illegible]	7 6 8	1015	2668	1469	492	66	10	3
Rahimganj	[illegible]	89216 10 12	30173 17 19	44328 12 10	[illegible]	[illegible]	40 12 1			377	2347	941	128	4		—
Kotebhajni	0	21809 7 9	5965 8 14	10855 16 5	4042 4 0	[illegible]	30 19 4	2 1 19	—	153	330	257	68	3	1	—
Teidhar	0	29506 16 19	8772 7 1	16624 2 17	3548 4 4	[illegible]	—			186	75	232	3	—		
Total	—	297265 3 18	83070 7 18	137991 5 18	[illegible]	[illegible]	[illegible] 5	47 1 17	7 6 8	2321	[illegible]	2008	692	103	13	1

Source: H.N. Choudhary, the Cooch Behar State and its land Revenue Settlement, p. 671.

APPENDIX - 5.I: Number of jotedars and undertenants and the land held by them MATHABHANGA

1	2	3	4	5	6	7	8	9	10	11	12	13	14	15	16	17
			Quantity of land Directly Head by							Jotes						
Name of Pargana	Name of Mahal	Total of assessed	Jotes	Chukans	Dar Chukans	Daradar Chukanis	Tasya Chukanis	Tail Chukanis	Tasya-Tail Chukanis	Number	Chukai	Dar-Chukanis	Daradar chukanis	Tasya-Chukanis	Tail-Chukanis	Tasya-Tail-Chukanis
Mekhliganj	[illegible]	344143 17 0	67640 13 1	147590 16 6	96236 4 17	31234 12 17	5374 5 3	918 10 13	148 14 3	2324	5268	4533	1861	402	75	10
Ditto	[illegible]	32257 2 5	1047 17 17	14006 15 0	9851 14 4	2290 5 14	61 5 10	...	—	160	439	448	117	7	—	—
Total		376400 19 5	68688 10 18	161596 11 6	106087 19 1	33525 2 11	5435 10 13	918 10 13	148 14 3	2484	5707	4981	1978	409	75	10
Banshkata Chhit	[illegible]	2774 10 10	571 5 5	1448 14 3	521 8 9	252 17 1	11 5 12		—	26	111	55	36	2	—	—
Maraghat Baishchala	[illegible]	2996 7 5	782 13 1	1648 12 16	746 6 0	118 15 9	29 19 16		—	19	32	25	6	1	—	
Total		382171 16 [illegible]	[illegible] 9 4	164[illegible] 18 6	107325 11 10	33907 15 1	5476 16 1	918 10 13	148 14 3	2529	5850	5061	2020	412	75	10

Source: H.N. Choudhary, the Cooch Behar State and its land Revenue Settlement, p. 672.

APPENDIX - 5.J: Number of jotedars and undertenants and the land held by them LALBAZAR AND DINHATA

1	2	3	4	5	6	7	8	9	10	11	12	13	14	15	16	17
			Quantity of land Directly Head by													
Name of Pargana	Name of Mehal	Total of assessed land	Jotes	Chukanis	Dar Chukanis	Daradar Chukanis	Tasya Chukanis	Tail Chukanis	Tasya-Tail Chukanis	Number of Jotes	Chukanis	Dar-Chukanis	Daradar chukanis	Tasya-Chukanis	Tail-Chukanis	Tasya-Tail-Chukanis
LALBAZAR																
		[illegible]	[illegible]	[illegible]	[illegible]	[illegible]	[illegible]	[illegible]	[illegible]							
Mekhliganj	[illegible]	281967 0 8	71726 18 17	161733 15 10	64061 11 19	12941 13 17	1446 16 11	65 18 5	—	2517	4945	3068	707	71	8	—
Ditto	[illegible]	5834 17 18	1932 3 14	2385 5 1	1164 19 19	122 3 4	—		—	87	161	78	17	—	..	—
Total		287801 18 6	73659 2 11	164349 0 11	65226 11 18	13064 8 1	1446 18 11	65 18 15	—	2604	5106	3146	724	71	8	—
[illegible]																
Dinhata	[illegible]	340891 16 10	58071 14 5	141492 8 6	105734 9 16	30014 15 7	5040 19 16	525 5 0	12 4 0	3720	10947	[illegible]723	4927	1085	127	8
Ditto	[illegible]	20707 16 14	3578 14 13	9422 4 8	6343 8 11	1492 8 11	162 18 18	7 1 5	—	790	772	686	233	36	1	—
Total		361599 13 4	61651 9 4	150914 12 14	[illegible] 18 9	31507 3 18	5203 18 14	532 6 5	12 4 0	[illegible]	[illegible]	[illegible]	5160	1121	128	8

Source: H.N. Choudhary, the Cooch Behar State and its land Revenue Settlement, p. 673.

APPENDIX - 5.k: Number of jotedars and undertenants and the land held by them COOCH BEHAR AND TUFANGANJ

1	2	3	4	5	6	7	8	9	10	11	12	13	14	15	16	17
Name of Pargana	Name of Meha	Total of assessed land	Quantity of land Directly Head by: Jotedars	Chukanis	Dar Chukanis	Daradar Chukanis	Tasya Chukanis	Tail Chukanis	Tasya-Tail Chukanis	Number of Jotes	Chukanis	Dar-Chukanis	Daradar chukanis	Tasya-Chukanis	Tail-Chukanis	Tasya-Tail-Chukanis
COOCHBEHAR																
		[illegible]	[illegible]	[illegible]	[illegible]	[illegible]	[illegible]	[illegible]	[illegible]							
Cooch Behar	[illegible]	436455 18 16	136,162 11 [illegible]	193399 12 5	84882 7 6	10832 6 5	2139 9 2	28 17 14	—	4451	9462	6024	1707	241	5	—
Ditto	[illegible]	72157 14 13	19270 4 2	35296 7 11	13943 9 [illegible]	3719 18 3	419 18 18	7 16 11	—	486	1216	882	274	56	1	—
Total	508613	13 9	155632 15 3	228695 19 19	98636 13 14	2,3352 4 8	2559 8 0	36 14 1	—	5337	10668	6806	1981	297	6	—
TUFANGANJ																
Tufan-ganj	[illegible]	242874 13 9	104126 18 0	97972 4 8	33127 8 6	6612 18 18	1035 3 17	—	—	1318	3387	1900	447	76	—	—
Ditto	[illegible]	43368 14 6	16013 2 10	17599 9 1	732 0 13	2234 15 16	322 6 6	—	—	387	920	328	112	18	—	—
Total		286244 [illegible] 15	120140 [illegible]	115571 13 4	40447 5 [illegible]	8847 14 14	1,137 10 3	—	—	2036	3507	2228	559	94	—	

Source: H.N. Choudhary, the Cooch Behar State and its land Revenue Settlement, p. 674.

Narayani Coins of Cooch Behar State

6

Experiencing Capital Investment

6.1 Non-agrarian Economy

Trade and commerce

In the accounts of Greek Merchants, dating from the first century AD brief reviews of trade and industry of that period had survived. The *'Tej – Patra'* (leaf of the Laurus leassia) of the *'Kiradia'* Country was exported to Europe from the port of Tamralipta. At annual fair Chinese merchants exchanged silks for *Tejpatra*. [1] Historian Bushell said that there was a trade between China and India through Burma and Assam from the fifth century B C. The center spot of trade between Bengal and Kamarupa was Hadira Chowki, now in district of Goalpara, Assam.[2] The Mohamedan historians have mentioned *oranges, black-pepper, fragrant flowers, fruits, guava, opium, ganjas* etc. as trade items. [3] They have also mentioned that the gold dust was collected from the sand of the Brahmaputra. Salt was not readily procurable and formerly pearl-oysters were found in the Karatoya river.[4]

Lawrence Mercer and John Lewis Chauvet were appointed by British Government to enquire all the matter regarding Cooch Behar. They also highlighted the condition of trade and commerce in Cooch Behar State.

TABLE –6.1

Quantity of imported and exported items of Cooch Behar State

Imported		*Exported*	
Commodity	*Quantity*	*Commodity*	*Quantity*
Salt	10,000	Rice	100000
Gaur	3000	Tobacco	40000
Iron	Small Quantity	Musterseeds	10000
		Opium	Small Quant

Source: Mercer and Chauvet Report, Cooch Behar Select Records, Vol-II, pp. 149-151.

All the evidences indicate the existence of a trading class in Cooch Behar at the time of 1596.[5] Miss Collet mentioned when Raja Rammohan Ray was the *Serestadar* of Rangpur (1809-1814), Marwary merchants met at night meeting. Huge number of Jains and Marwaries trading Community lived there.[6] Radha Krishna Bairagi mentioned "*Kaiya Banik*" in his book ***'Gosaini Mangal***. [7] Marwary people here called ***Kaiya***. According to Bhabani Charan Bandhyopadhya, most of the trading classes came from Jodhpur, Bikanir, Murshidabad, Delhi, Kanpur, Gujrat etc. [8] According to W.W. Hunter, "nearly all the Commerce of the State except such as is carried on at the weekly markets is in the hands of foreign merchants, chiefly Marwaris from Bikanir. Who bring more energy and enterprise to the work than the Kuch Beharis usually possess". [9]

The migration of the trading class had been so thorough, that the political Agents were surprised to see that there was not a single class of people among the subjects of the Maharaja who were by profession traders. As a result, the entire trade and commerce of Cooch Behar State in the late 19th century, was in the hands of British subjects. The traders of neighbouring districts controlled both the import and export trade of the state. These traders enjoyed complete freedom in carrying on their trade and were treated with great consideration by the administration of the State.

Market

Cooch Behar town was very important place of business. There was two important ***Bazar*** in Cooch Behar *Town* – ***Calicagunj Bazar*** and ***Toha Bazar*** (present name, Bhawaniganj Bazar). [10] Besides these, there were also so many ***Bunders*** and ***Hats*** scattered all over the State. The *Bunders* were the seats of trade and commerce where merchants permanently resided and had firms for the conduct of business. Mainly the *Bunders* were situated on big rivers, or by the side of public roads and command a large amount of traffic, both in word and out word. Primarily, *Bunder* was called a *Hat*. But the latter grow in importance, it began to draw larger traffic, and if the site was favourable with good means of communication by land or by water an experimental shop was opened by the side of the *Hat* by some enterprising men. With the spread of business, the space around the *Hat* was gradually filled up and it became the *Bunder*. The place soon grew into a little rural town. The Bunders transformed in to a busy place of trade.[11]

The number of important Bunders in the State was twenty-five. [12] Haldibari was the largest and by far the most important Bunder of Cooch Behar State. Other important Bunders were – Mekhliganj, Mathabhanga, Fulbari, Dinhata, Dewanhat, Kholta, Gosanimari, Shitai, Balarampur, Ghoramara, Natabari, Lalkuthi, Mahishkuchi, Maranga, Changrabandha etc.[13] A Hat was a public place of business lying with rural area, where people of the neighbourhood assemble on the days of the week for the purpose of buying and selling things of everyday use and mostly of local production. The site fixed for a Hat was generally shady and lies by the side of a public road or way. Things were brought to the Hat in ***carts or bhars***. A *bhar* was a flat piece of bamboo placed across the shoulder with a load suspended from either end by means of a rope, in when the men used the ***bhar***.[14] The commodities offered for sale were, rice, paddy, vegetables, dal, fish, oil, salt, sugar, sweets, dahi or card and *chura* etc. The average daily attendance varies from 100 to 3000 according to the importance of the ***Hat***. Most of the Hats usalluy assembled at about 2 O'Clock in the after noon and stayed till nightfall.[15]

The total numbers of *Hats* in the State was 119 scattered in 1,204 Taluks with a total area of 1307 square miles. The proprietory right to the Hats vested directly in the state and it was leased out by auction to the highest bidder for a term of years. So Hats were important for internal trade of the State.

Annual Fairs

Besides markets, regular annual fairs were organized at the seven major towns of the State - Cooch Behar, Tufanganj, Dinhata, Sitai, Mathabhanga, Mekhliganj and Haldibari. The most important was, of course, the fair of ***Rasyatra*** of Cooch Behar. It was held every winter (November – December) and lasted for 15 days; it was largely attended (Probably 30,000 people). [16] They came from neighbouring district, and State like – Rangpur, Bagura, Dacca, Assam, Manipur etc. [17] Next in importance was the fair of ***Doljatra*** at Tufanganj town and it also lasted for 15 days. The large number of people (probably 2,500 people) assembled in *Doljatra* fair from different parts of the State. In this fair, articles to the value of Rs. 5000 and more were sold in one day.

TABLE –6.2

Important Fairs of Cooch Behar State

Place	*Time Bengali month*	*Occasion*	*Duration*	*Attendence*
Phalimari	Aswin (October)	Durgapuja	7 days	1500
Gopalpur	Phalgun (February)	Sivaratri	5 days	2000
Angarkata	Phalgun (February)	Dolyatra	5 days	5000
Cooch Behar	Kartic (October)	Rasyatra	15 days	30000
Balabhut	Aswin (October)	Durgapuja	5 days	4000-5000
Bhandigalas	Kartic (October)	Rasyatra	15 days	400

Tfanganj town	Phalgun (February)	Dolyatra	15 days	2500
Khalisa Gosanimari	Aswin	Durgapuja	5 days	2000
Brahmanir chowki	Kartic (October)	Kalipuja	7 days	2500
Simulbari	Magh-Phalgun (February-March)	Sannyasi Thakurer Mela	1 Month	10000-12000
Chaora hat	Paush (December)	Sankrantir Mela	2 Months	500
Mahamaya path	Aswin	Durgapuja	5 days	500
Dinhata	Phalgun	Sivaratri	7 days	5000
Bhogmara	Paush	Paush Mela	7 days	4000-5000
Changra-bandha	Agrahayan	Changra-bandha Mela	1 Month	5000
Jamaldaha	Chaitra	Barani Snan	1 Month	

Source: Durgadas Majumdar, *West Bengal District Gazetteers*, Koch Behar, pp. 106-13.

Import Trade

The principal articles of impartance were the following: *Salt, Dry chillis, Gur, Sugar, Brass, Copper utensils, Molasses, pulses, Spices, Cocoa-nuts, Betel-nuts, beads, dry fish, kerosene oil, wheat, Cloths, Rang, Cotton European Liquor opium, Ganja piece* etc.

There was no import duty of any kind in the state. Almost all the articles were brought from the neighbouring state and districts. The European Liquor was generally imported from Calcutta or Dacca, while opium from the neighbouring district.[18] Dry fish was in great demand and a brisk trade was carried on in it all the year round. The wheat was chiefly used by the men who had been in the service of the Maharaja. The kerosene oil, piece-cloth, umbrella, and other fancy things also gradually began to enter into the interior of the state since the middle of 19th century.

The total value of import trade must have been considerable. According to W.W. Hunter the total estimate of imports in per annum was £ 90000 in 1872.[19] But no statistics was ever maintained by the state officials from which this value could be ascertained.

Export Trade

The chief articles of export were the following: Tobacco, Jute, Musterd-oil, Rice, Forest products (timbers, thatching grass, canes, bamboos etc.). The most important export items were Tobacco and Jute, which were grown in aboundance in the cultivation. The Tobacco and Jute were exported to the neighbouring districts and also to the European countries. [20] Timber, bamboos, canes etc. were exported to the neighbouring Brtitish Districts. Before the opening of railway, nearly the whole of both inward and out ward traffic used to be carried on by country-boats. The railways had considerably diverted the traffic and have almost monopolized the export of Jute. The chief Jute – exporting stations were *Haldibari, Changrabandha, Chawrahat, Mathabhanga* and the town of *Cooch Behar*; the principal tobacco centers were *Mekhlganj*, Mathabhanga, Shibpurbawra, Gosanimari and Chawrahat and the principal marts dealing in mustard-seeds and musterd-oil were Balarampur, Tufanganj, Ghoramara, Natabari, Ambari, Maruganj and Mahishkuchi.[21]

TABLE –6.3

Name of the Articles	*Extent of Export*	
	Amount maunds	*Value*
Tobacco	4,00,000	20,00,000
Jute	3,00,000	12,00,000
Mustard seed	25,000	1,00,000
Total	7,25,000	33,00,000

Source: Durgadas Majumdar, *West Bengal District Gazetteers*, Koch Behar, pp.97-98.

In the absence of statistics, the amount and value of

the export trades of the country cannot be categorically stated. The extent of the export trade may be roughly estimated as below –

Manufactured Products

The Cooch Behar state was once famous for its manufactured products. All sorts of articles made of Silk, cotton, Jute, bamboo, wood were manufactured in the State. There were Weavers, Goldsmiths, Blacksmiths, Carpenters, Washermen and others. [22] The items especially prepared were the following -

i) Silk-Fabrics

A kind of rough and coarse silk was obtained from the endi worm, which was regularly reared for this purpose. These cloths were 24 inches wide and 9 feet long and these were used in winter period. The industry was confined to women and the market value was almost nothing. The ***endi-cloth*** was prepared mostly for personal wear. Cheap foreign cloths were, however, superior to these articles of native manufacture.[23]

ii) Cotton Fabrics

During the pre-British period, the people of Cooch Behar State used to wear homemade clothes. But after that, when the State began the import of foreign cloths, the native industry completely died out and then the weavers began to make cloths of the kinds known as fota and patani, both plain and coloured, mostly worn by the females. [24] The ***gamcha*** or napkins were prepared by the native tantis were comparatively in demand.

iii) Jute Fabrics

Mekhli and gunny are prepared from jute in different parts of the country, especially in the west, and there is still a brisk market for it. The finest production from jute was the mekhli as the colored jutecolths of Mekhliganj.[25]

There was large number of people who got involved in different manufacturing producing industry. The natives were born artists. They made stools, cots, moras and chairs, pipes, sunshades, sandals, fans, fine mats from bamboos and woods. The gold smiths or *banias* made silver-ornaments, necklace, mootha, foot or ear ring, noth or nose ring etc. Ghee, mustard oil, molasses were produced in Cooch Behar State. The State produced the best quality mustard oil in the whole Bengal. The large quantity of oil was exported to the districts of eastern Bengal by the merchants.

Labour

One of the peculiar features of the population structure of late 19the century of Cooch Behar was the absence of a distinct body of day labourers. When labourer was available there were some works, which a native would not do. Digging and carrying of soil were the foremost of these. For these works, the services of up-country Coolies had always to be needed. It was the domestic servants, farm labourers, and carpenters, who generally contributed their labour. The wages differed almost in every case, and were changed both by month and year.

TABLE – 6.4: Some Wage Structure in Cooch Behar State has been given below

Name of service	*wages per dien*			*wages per mensen*				
	Rs		*As*	*Rs.*	*As*		*Rs.*	*As*
Domestic Servants	...		....	1	8	to	4	0
Farm Labourer	5	to	6	....				
Digger		4					7	8
Thatcher.		-				-		
Ordinary	4	to	5	7	8	to	9	8
Expert	6	to	8	10	0	to	15	0
Carpenter	6	to	8	10	0	to	15	0

Source: Durgadas Majumdar, *West Bengal District Gazetteers*, Koch Behar, p. 97.

The domestic servants had to be paid monthly. The native servants agreed to work on yearly wages. In most of the cases the labourers worked on monthly wages or yearly wages.

Prices of Agriculture Crops

The main crops grown in the Cooch Behar State were ***aman*** and ***aus* rice**, Jute, Tobacco, mustard seeds, pulses, wheat, millets, kaon, makai (Indian corn), sugar cane and vegetables. [26] The names of the principal crops cultivated in the Cooch Behar State, the time of cultivation, and market price of crops are given below-

TABLE – 6.5

Principal Crops and Market Price of Crops

Name of crops	*Time of cultivation*	*Average outturn & Bigha in months*	*Average value & mound* Rs.	A	P
Haimanti paddy	May to August	6 months	2	0	0
Bitri paddy	Feb to march	7½ months	2	0	0
Tobacco	Sept to nov.	5 months	5	0	0
Potato	Do	12 months	1	4	0
Jute	April	5 months	4	0	0
Mustard oil	October	1 months	4	0	0
Til	August	1	4	0	0
Wheat	Oct. to nov	6	2	3	0
Barley	Do	6	2	8	0
China	January	6	1	8	0
Kaon	Do	8	2	0	0
Pulses	Aug. to sept.	3	3	0	0
Arhar	April	3		-	
-	Some	-		-	

Source: *Census Report 1961, Government of West Bengal District Census Hand Book, Cooch Behar.*

Of all the crops tobacco was the most profitable. Next important crop was jute. Among the paddies the ***Bitri*** brought in a great income that the ***Haimanti,*** mustard seeds earned very little income. Tobacco and jute trade was thus more prosperous than that of the mustard seed.

The magnitudes relating to yield rates (production per unit of land, hence on bighas) of the crops cultivated and harvested by the peasants from the agricultural fields of this territory were not available chronologically in the form of historical time series for the region of Rajas. Owing to this, table containing the data relating to yield rates of the crops of this place for the period, 1871–1872 to 1949–1950 has been constructed with large information vacuum. However, the table amply allows one to state that the yield rates of paddy, jute and tobacco, the major crops of this place were not noticeably high during the stated period. Again the same table clearly demonstrates that the yield rates of *paddy* and jute declined in the same period. Yield rates in quintals per bigha of different crops in the Cooch Behar State-

TABLE – 6.6: Yearwise Rates of Crops have been given below

Name of the crops	*1871–1872 yield Rates*	*1903–1904 yield Rates*	*1949 – 1950 yield Rates*
Paddy	2.61	2.50	1.52
Jute	NA	1.86	1.58
Tobacco	NA	1.86	NA

Source: *Census Report 1961, West Bengal District Census Hand Book, Cooch Behar.*

Multiple cropping practices were not an exceptional phenomenon in Cooch Behar during this period. In this place, it was very much prevalent at that time. Although the idea about its extent for the period 1871–1872 to 1949–1950 could not be had on account of unavailability of relevant quantitative information, the principal or common manner of it can be understood from same qualitative information presented in the following excerpt: "Something two crops of rice, one of aus and one of aman, are obtained from the same land during the year; sometime also pulses are show on aman rice land in October and November shortly before the winter rice harvest, the pulses growing after the rice has been cut. China, a species of millet and kaon are also occasionally sown after the reaping of the aman arop; and aus rice is often grown as a seeond crop on land from which a crop of mustard seed has been already taken".[27]

6.2 Agrarian Economy

The kingdom of Kamata –Koch Behar was pre-eminently agricultural since the dawn. The main source of income of Cooch Behar State was the land revenue. Large portion of people was dependent on agriculture. When Anglo-Koch treaty was concluded, in1773, the British entered in to the state and their first target was to improve the agrarian economy as early as possible. The corps raised by the people in this state may be divided in to the following five main groups. [28]

Food grains

1. Paddy a) *Bitri* b) *Haimanti*

2.Wheat 3. Barley 4. China 5. Kaon 6. Pulses (variety type) 7. Makai

Oil seeds

1.Mustard seeds 2. Til

Tobacco

Manufactural Crops:

1. Jute 2. Shan 3. Reah 4. Sugar cane 5. Mootha.

Roots and Bulbs

1. Potato 2. Onion 3. Garlic 4. Kadroo 5. Ada 6. Hatood

All these crops are raised in every part of the state more or less degree. The principal crops of the State were *Paddy, Tobacco, Jute, Mustard seeds*.

Paddy

a) *Bitri Paddy*

There were two Bitri crops early and late. The first crop

was seen at the beginning of Magh or middle of January and gathering began in June. The second crop was seen at the beginning in February and harvesting started in July or August. The total area where *Bitri* paddy grew was 255000 Bighas as distributed below-

TABLE – 6.7: Cultivated Land has increased in different Parganas

Name of Parganas	*Extent of early Bitri cultivation in Bighas*	*Extent of ordinary Bitri cultivation in Bighas*	*Total extent of Bitri cultivation in Bighas*
Mekhliganj	3000	35000	38000
Mathabhanga	3900	37000	34900
Dinhata	2500	39000	41500
Haldibari	5000	34000	39000
Cooch Behar	4600	57000	61600
Tufanganj	2000	38000	40000
Total =	21000	234000	255000

Source: S.C. Ghosal, *A History of Cooch Behar*, 1942, p. 45.

The total production of the entire State there fore was upto about 1912500 mounds. The value of this amount was about 33,46,875 rupees. The figures of the different Parganas are given below -

TABLE – 6.8: Value and Market Price has been given below:

Name of Parganas	*Total produce in Maunds*	*Total value in Rupees*
Mekhliganj	261750	458063
Mathabhanga	285500	498750
Lalbazar	352250	544687
Dinhata	251000	511875
Cooch Behar	462000	808500
Tufanganj	300000	525000
Total =	1912500	33,46,875

Source: H.N. Chaudhury, *The Cooch Behar State and its Land Revenue Settlement*, 1903, p. 75.

b) Haimanti Paddy

There were two methods of the cultivation of ***Haimanti*** paddy. One was by at once sowing the seeds like the ***betri*** and other by first rearing the seedlings in separate piece of land and then transplanting them in the field. The total area of the cultivarion of the Haimanti paddy was about twice the extent of the Bitri cultivation, as detailed below-

TABLE – 6.9: Cultivation of Haimanti Paddy in Different Parganas

Name of Parganas	*Extent of Haimanti cultivation in Bighas*
Mekhliganj	75000
Mathabhanga	95000
Lalbazar	60000
Dinhata	120000
Cooch Behar	115000
Tufanganj	59000
Total =	524000

Source: H.N.Chaudhury, *The Cooch Behar State and its Land Revenue Settlement, 1903*, pp. 176-179.

The throughout of Haimanti paddy was less than of bitri, and varied from 4 to 8 Maunds a Bigha. The figures for the production and value of this crop for the different parganas are given below-

TABLE – 6.10: Production and Market Value of Crops in Cooch Behar State

Name of Parganas	*Produce in Maunds*	*Value in Rupees*
Mekhliganj	450000	787500
Mathabhanga	570000	997500
Lalbazar	360000	630000
Dinhata	720000	1260000
Cooch Behar	690000	1207500
Tufanganj	354000	619500
Total =	3144000	5502000

Source: District Census Hand Book, 1951, Cooch Behar, p. 52.

The people of Cooch Behar were dependent upon rice as food. It could be seen that no protion of rice was to be exported

Tobacco

It is one of the principal crops of the State and that was proftable of all agricultural products of the people. Lalbazar was especially famous for the excellence of its tobacco. This crop was also very largely raised in Mekhliganj, Mathabhanga, and Dinhata and formed one of the staple agriculture products of those parganas. The *traffic* in tobacco was large and the people made a great deal of money by it. Tobacco was sent by boats to the neighbouring districts of Bengal in large quantities. [29] The Burmese merchants annually took away thousands and thousands of tobacco from Mekhliganj and Lalbazar.

The species of tobacco were growing in the state: ordinary and ***hamakoo***. Cultivation of hamakoo was extensive in Mekhliganj. The people did not know how to cure the leaves. The knowledge of tobacco curing would be of immense benefit to the State which grew excellent tobacco and in large quantities. The table given below shows the area of tobacco cultivation:(1900 AD)

TABLE – 6.11: Tobacco Cultivation and Quantities have been given below

Name of Parganas	*First class*	*Second class*	*Third class*	*Total*
Mekhliganj	1474	5220	5097	11791
Mathabhanga	7477	15276	8624	31377
Lalbazar	17935	8695	3080	29710
Dinhata	2867	5484	3610	11991
Cooch Behar	3364	7545	9035	19944
Tufanganj	36	107	942	1085
Total =	33153	42327	30418	105898

Source: W. W.Hunter, *A Statistical Account of Bengal*, Vol-X, p. 104.

For the practical purposes 105898 bighas might had been taken annualy for the cultivation of tobacco. The production, values and net profits of cultuvatiors are given below-

TABLE 6.12: Production and Values of Tobacco in Cooch Behar State

Name of Parganas	*Production of tobacco in maunds*	*Value in Rupees*	*Cultivatiors net profit in Rupees*
Mekhliganj	55000	275,000	137500
Mathabhanga	155000	275000	387500
Lalbazar	145000	725000	362500
Dinhata	60000	300000	150000
Cooch Behar	100000	500000	250000
Tufanganj	5000	25000	12500
Total =	520000	2600000	1300000

Source: *Annual Administrative Report of Cooch Behar State*, 1900-1901, p.42.

Maharaja Kumar Jitetndra Narayan wrote in a book in 1915 on the subject of tobacco. He wrote, "Tobacco is a principal crop of Cooch Behar; and with a view to introduce in the state scientific methods of curing as followed is other countries, under the instruction of my father His late Highness Maharaja Sir Nripendra Narayan Bhup Bahadur, (1863-1911) I went to Cornell university, New Yourk, where I specialized in agriculture for sometime; and to Cuba, West Indies, where I observed the method of the culture, curing and manufacture of the famous tobacco. Mr. Mazumdar (I. B. Mazumdar) was deputed by my father to accompany me in my tours, and to specialize in tobacco; the later visited the different tobacco growing centres in Macedonia and Asia Minor, where the best Turkish tobacco comes from".[30]

The experimental tobacco Farms at Nilkuthi and at Dinhata were started in 1905-06.[31] Two hundred and seventy six Bighas of land were included in the Nilkuthi Farms and twenty Bighas in the Dinhata Farm. The annual grant for the maintenance of the two Farms was Rs. 18,000. The varieties of tobacco tried and grown in the farm were Virginian or American, Turkish and Cubian. The result in all cases had been successful and expert opinion had pronounced that the quality of the tobacco grown in the State farms was almost as good as grown in America. The highest price obtained was Rs. 60 per mound and the lowest price was Rs 25, while the average price per *mound* of State tobacco was Rs. 12 only. In July, 1912, Dinhata farm was the centre of the chief tobacco area in the State.[32]

Jute

Jute was one of the principal crops of the people of the State. It was largely grown in every part of the State. The Jute grown in the State had been fine fiber and was demand in Calcutta. The total area of Jute cultivation land of the whole State is given below-

TABLE – 6.13: Cultivation of Jute in Cooch Behar State

Name of Parganas	*Extent of cultivation of Jute in Bighas*
Mekhliganj	13000
Mathabhanga	10000
Lalbazar	9000
Dinhata	14000
Cooch Behar	12000
Tufanganj	7000
Total =	65000

Source: I.B. Mazumdar, *How to improve Tobacco in India*, 1915, p. 40.

The out turn of a bigha of Jute varied from 4 to 6 maunds, giving an average of 5 maunds and the value of a maund was between Rs. 3 and Rs. 5. The figures have been given below showing the total production and values -

TABLE – 6.14

Production and Values of Jute in Cooch Behar State

Name of Parganas	Produce in Maunds	Value in Rupees
Mekhliganj	65000	260000
Mathabhanga	50000	200000
Lalbazar	45000	180800
Dinhata	70000	280000
Cooch Behar	60000	240000
Tufanganj	35000	140000
Total =	325000	1300000

Source: *Annual Administrative Report of Cooch Behar State,* 1911-1912, p. 35.

Mustard seeds

Mustard seed was one of the staple crops of Parganas. The gross production of a bigha of mustard seeds was 3 or 4 maunds. The area and the value are given below -

TABLE – 6.15

Cultivation of Mustard Seeds and Quantities have been given below

Name of Parganas	Extent of cultivation in Bighas	Total produces (maunds)
Mekhliganj	3000	4500
Mathabhanga	4000	6000
Lalbazar	3000	4500
Dinhata	5000	7500
Cooch Behar	13000	19500
Tufanganj	12000	18000
Total =	40000	60000

Source: H. N. Chaudhury, *Cooch Behar State and its Land Revenue Settlement,* Cooch Behar,1903, p.77.

NOTES AND REFERENCES

1. S. C. Ghosal, *A History of Cooch Behar*, Cooch Behar, 1942, p. 58.
2. *Ibid*, p. 59.
3. H. N. Chaudhury, *The Cooch Behar State And its Land Revenue Settlement*, 1903, pp. 156-157.
4. *Ibid.*, p. 158.
5. Kalyan Das, *Jalpaiguri Marwaries Society Prosange Kichu Katha*, p. 20.
6. Miss Collet, *Life and Letters of Ranmohan Ray*, 1900, p.344.
7. Radha Krishna Das Bairagi, *Gosani Mangal* (ed), Nripendra Nath Paul, 1978, p. 27.
8. W. W. Hunter, *A Statistical Account of Bengal*, Vol. X, p. 398.
9. Ajitesh Bhattacharjee, *Madhuparni*, Special Cooch Behar Sankha (Bengali), 1990, p. 179.
10. *Ibid.*, pp. 179-180.
11. H. N. Chaudhury, *op. cit.*, p. 180.
12. Durgadas Majumdar, *West Bengal District Gazetteers*, Kooch Behar, 1977, p. 97.
13. H. N. Chaudhury, *op.cit.*, p. 71.
14. *Ibid*, p.74.
15. *Annual Administrative Report of Cooch Behar State*, 1874, p. 95.
16. *Ibid*, p. 97.
17. H. N. Chaudhury, *op.cit.*, p. 75.
18. W. W. Hunter, *op.cit.*, pp. 398-399.
19. H. N. Chaudhury, *op.cit.*, p. 193.
20. *Ibid*, pp. 193-194.
21. *Loc.cit*.
22. S.C. Ghosal, *op.cit.*, p. 91.
23. H. N. Chaudhury, *op.cit.*, pp. 194-195.

24. W. W. Hunter, *op.cit.*, p. 396.
25. H. N. Chaudhury, *op.cit.*, p. 157.
26. Government of West Bengal Census 1961, West Bengal District Census Hand Book, Cooch Behar, p. 115
27. Bhagabati Charan Bandopadhya, *A History of Cooch Behar* (Bengali), Cooch Behar, 1882, p. 64.
28. Final Settlement Report (1913-1927), Cooch Behar, p. 53.
29. Ajitesh Bhattacharjee, *op.cit.*, p. 208.
30. *Annual Administrative Report of Cooch Behar State*, 1910-1911, p.45.
31. *Ibid*, 1915-1916, p.42.
32. I. B. Mazumdar, *How to Omprove Tobacco in India*, 1915, p. Introduction.

7

The British and The Cooch Behar State in the Decade before Partition

The period between 1937 to 1947 is described as the decade of destiny in the history of the Indian freedom movement. Some momentous decisions and momental declarations were made during this period that determined the course of national movement, the inevitable document of which was both trumph and tragedy for the people of the Subcontinent. The British Government wanted to introduce the Fedaration of India in 1935 to the Princely States. Viceroy Linlithgo said to the Rajas and Maharajas of Princely State that "when I last had the honour of addressing your Highness, I referred to the steps which I had taken to assist the individual Rulers in reading a decision in regard to the Federation of India. It has taken longer than I could have noted to clear the ground and to examine the numerous points, points of varying importance, rose by the individual Rulers in one connection or another with the Federal offer. But that work is now completed. The points advanced for consideration by the Rulers of the Indian states, with out exception, been examined, and the Federal offer, framed in the light of a close and objection examination of those points has now been drawn up and communicated to the States...........I am content now to await the verdict of the Rulers".[1]

In the mean time, the British Government took a liberal policy and to invite the rulers of princely State to join the Federal Legislature. The British Government declared the political and administrative reforms of princely States "As your Highness have lately been assured, the paramount power stands ready to support the princes in the fulfilment of its treaty obligations. That does not, I need not say, for a moment mean the princes themselves are not the primary custodians of their ancient and illustrions heritages. How often has it not been impressed on the princes of India by those who have had their best interests at heart that they should sink their differences and stand shoulder to shoulder for the good of their States and for their own happiness and peace of mind?.........In no case is the need for co-operation and combination more patent, more pronounced, and more immediate than in the case of the smaller states". [2] Jawaharlal Neheru opposed the British policy to princely States and he said to the 'All India States Peoples Conference' "we are told now of the so-called independence of the States and their treaties with the paramount power, which are sacrosanct and inviolable and apparently must go on for ever and ever". [3]

The mentality had changed when the scheme of Federation with British India materialised. Though unlimited powers were reserved to the Indian Rulers in the proposed scheme of federation, the times had so much changed that it would not be possible for any ruler to exercise these powers. The public opinion had great force and willingly or unwillingly the authorities had to reject it.[4] According to Bhulabhai Desai, "we next turned to the present Act of 1935 and to the question of Federation. I pointed out to him that if particularly nullified even a small measure of responsible government in the provinces and that as those who lead the democratic party would have very limited scope for measures of public good or advancement and that as even in that limited sphere the princes, representatives were bound to be a serious obstacle, we were rightly opposed to the Federation as contemplated.

The only thing he the viceroy had to say in favour of the Federation was that if would be an act of kindness, if not duty, towards the subjects of the Indian states to have federation, because it was the only way by which the personal autocritic rule would, with our much effort and loss of time, be replaced by better conditions in the states".[5]

In 1939-1940, Maharaja of Cooch Behar, Jagaddipendra Narayan attended so many Conferences organized by Chamber of Princes and the subject was to discuss the State joint Fedaral of India. One of the important facts was that the Maharaja of Cooch Behar always wanted to maintain good relation with the British Government. The outbreak of the Second World War was another occasion to override normal political authority of State. Bound contractually, the Maharaja had the need to prove His loyalty in the historic task. As soon as His Majesty's Government was in war with Germany on the 3rd September 1939, the Maharaja placed his personal services and the entire resources of the State and its disposal. Towards the years 1939-40 the State's involvement was to the monetary donations to the war purposes Fund. The Durbar's war contributions during the year to the various Funds were as follows.[6]

1. His Excellency the Viceroy's war Fund ——— 30000
2. Indian Red Cross Society ——— 5000
3. St. John's Ambulance Association ——— 5000
4. St. Dunstan's Association ——— 5000

==========

Total = 45000

On September 2, 1939 'The Cooch Behar Registration of Foreigners order' was promulgated and issued in the State of Cooch Behar. On 3rd September, Government declared Emergency over the State, 6th September, "Defence of India Ordinance" was declared. Notification of Viceroy of India about war situation, the State of Cooch Behar spread the notification over the State —"In these days when the whole of cvilisation is threatened, the widespread attachment of India to the cause in which we have taken up arms has been a source of deep satisfaction to me. I also value most highly the mony and generous offers of assistance made to me by the princes and people of India. I am confident that in the struggle upon which my people and I have now entered we can count on sympathy and support from every quarter of the Indian continent in the face of the common ddanger. Britain is fighting for no selfish ends but for the maintence of a principle vital to the future of mankind-the principle that relations between civilized states must be regulated not by force but by reason and law, so that men may live free from the terror of war to pursue the happiness and well-being which should be the destiny of mankind. Signed. George, R I". [7]

The Maharaja of Cooch Behar notified to form "Village 'Defence party' to protect of the internal affairs of the State on 30th September, 1940. The main activity of the Defence party was– **1)** to assist the local police generally in the protection of the civil population against *goondaism* and out break of crime as a sequel to war conditions. For this purpose the party took some measures as under:

a) To organise according to necessity night and also day petrols in the populated localities, *hats* and *bundars* and communicate with the local police if anything suspicious was found. b) To attend Railway stations, ferry ghats, etc to detect arrivals of suspicious persons and foreigners and when any was detected, to inform the police forth with c) To rest to an event of an alarm or out break of fire they should immediately proceed in a body to the spot and render necessary help d) To arrest criminals when they found them in the actual Commission of crime and pursue escaping criminals to fix their identity and residence. **2)** To assist in every way possible all efforts in furtherance of successful prosecution of the war and maintenance of internal peace and tranquility. Such assistance would include. (a) helping in the circulation of accurate war news (b) by their own calm bearing to allay public panic caused by rumours (c) counteracting any effort of unscrupulous or designing persons to disseminate disloyalty or stir up communal discord".[8]

In the mean time, Maharaja Jagaddipendra Narayan passed the Cooch Behar Legislative Council Act 1941.The Legislative Council was consisted of-

1. His Highness the Maharaja of Bhup Bahadur as the President.

2. Ex-officio Members, viz-the Ministers of the State including the Chief Minister.

3. Elected Members viz-

a) Two non-official Members (one Hindu and one Mahomedan elected by the Jotedars of the State)

b) One Member elected by the Members of the legal profession of the State

c) Five non-official Members elected-one by each of the five sub-divisions of the State, namely -Sadar, Dinhata, Mathabhanga, Mekhliganj and Tufanganj

4) Nominated members viz-

a) One to represent the *Rajgunj* of the State;

b) One to represent commerce and industry in the State;

c) Additional Members not exceeding five in numbers appointed by His Hisghness the Maharaja.[9]

It is right to say that the reign of Maharaja Jagaddipendra Narayan (1922-1949), maintained good relation with the Paramount power. After the end of 2nd world war, the political scenario began to change redically and Naval Mutiny was started in 1946. In this situation, British Prime Minister Clement Atlee sent Cabinet Mission to discuss the planning of British India and Indian States. The Cabinet Mission's plan was to form federation with British India and Princely States. They also promised "there was no intention of making proposals for the entry of States into the Indian set up on any basis, other than that of negotiations".[10] The Mission was more emphatic on the independent character of Indian Princely States–"the rights of the States flowed from their relationships with the Crown, and would no longer exist, and that the rights surrendered by the States to the paramount power would revert to them. It was optional for the States to enter into any kind of relationship with the successor Government or Governments in British India, or to make an arrangement between themselves".[11]

In the post Second World War period, there was a rapid change of the political scenario of India and Bengal. A Cabinet Mission formed by British Prime Minister, Clement Atlee under the leadership of Lord Pathic Lowrence, Sir Stafford Cripps and A.V. Alexander planned to form a Federal State along with the Native States on 23rd March, 1946 inaction to the reformation of the Wavel's policy of 1945.[12] Lord Wavel, the Viceroy of India declared India to allow equal representation of the main communities to the Executive Committee.But the doubt arose among the communities in the policy of Bi-racial programme of Lord Wavel. The policy was about to rouse the separate feeling of the Hindus and the Muslims. Mharaja Jagaddipendra Narayan understood his own position in the changing situation along with other kings of Native States. The British authority was thinking at this period to transfer power to India.[13]

The Hitasadhani Sabha was established in Cooch Behar State in 1946, though the Maharaja was not the president of the Hitasadhani Sabha. According to the convention and practice of the Princely State, the King or Queen would be the Head or president of every organization. But it is noteworthy that the encouragement and sympathy of the king was indirectly expressed in favour of the Cooch Behar Hitasadhani Sabha.[14] The *Hitasadhani Sabha* was more emphatic on the development of the inhabitant of Cooch Behar or Sons of the soil or *Cooch Beharies*. The first concrete historical evidence was the Election of 1946 of the Cooch Behar State.TheHitasadhani Sabha had participated in both the elections and got thumping majority in the legislative Council of the Cooch Behar State.[15]

Maharaja Jagaddipendra Narayan was truly the well wisher of the Native inhabitants. He was busy for making the people conscious of the developmental works of the kingdom. In the mean time H.J. Tod, Resident of Eastern Estates advised King Jagaddipendra Narayan to form a separate administrative structure of independent Cooch Behar on 3rd April, 1947.[16] On 3rd June, 1947 the British Govt. declared the decision of power to India by dividing India and making another State named Pakisthan.[17] Jawaharlal Nehru, Prime Mnister optnioned to connect the Native States with the neighbouring big Provinces. As a result, the grievances of the Native States began to accrue; Cooch Behar king was also thoughtful of the situation.

The State of Cooch Behar was fully independent State upto 1949; the State did not join both India and Pakisthan. But after Maharaja was interested to join in India on 28th of August, 1949, an Agreement was signed between the Governor General of India and His Highness, the Maharaja of Cooch Behar, which came to be known as the Cooch Behar Merger Agreement. In this famous merger agreement, His Highness, the Maharaja of Cooch Behar ceded to the Dominion Government (Government of India) "full and exclusive authority, jurisdiction and powers for and in relation to the governance of the State" and agreed "to transfer the administration of the State to the Dominion Government on the 12th day of September, 1949". [18] Finally Cooch Behar State became the (1st January, 1950) district of West Bengal.[19] This is another interesting episode, the Cooch Behar State and this is being sidelined because it is not within the purview of the present dissertation.

NOTES AND REFERENCES

1. S. R. Ashton, *British policy towards the Indian States (1905-1939)*, London, 1982, p. 140.
2. *Ibid.*, p. 204.

3. Barbara N. Ramusack, *The Indian princes and their States,* Cambrige University Press, 2004, p. 264.
4. *Annual Administrative Report of Cooch Behar State,* 1940-41, pp. 3-4.
5. *The Cooch Behar Gazette,* Cooch Behar, 1934, p. 10.
6. *Annual Administrative Report of Cooch Behar State, 1940-41,* pp. 5-6.
7. *The Cooch Behar Gazette,* Cooch Behar, 1941, p.12.
8. P.N. Chopra (ed), *Towards Freedom 1937-47,* Vol-I, 1985, New Delhi, pp. 290-293.
9. *Ibid.,* p. 937.
10. V. P. Menon, *The Transfer of Power, 1942-1947,* Vol. II, 1972, London, p. 126.
11. *Ibid,* p. 134.
12. Suniti Kumar Ghosh, *India and the Raj (1919-1947),* 1989, Calcutta, p. 330.
13. Lumby, E.W.R., *The Transfer of Power, 1945-1947,* London, 1954, p. 219.
14. *Annual Administrative Report of Cooch Behar State,* Cooch Behar, 1946, p. 12.
15. *The Cooch Behar Gazette,* Cooch Behar, 1946, p. 32.
16. *Ibid.,* p. 42.
17. D.A. Low (ed), *Congress and the Raj: Facets of the Indian Struggle 1917-1947,* London, 1977, p. 204.
18. Kumud R. Biswas, *West Bengal District Gazetteers,* Calcutta, 1999, p. 217.
19. *Ibid.,* p. 219.

8

Conclusion

A critical study of the British rule in the Cooch Behar state shows that the pattern of administration established was what today is often called "Indirect Rule". In Cooch Behar State, it was applied as early as the East India Company's contact with this state in 1773, when Anglo-Koch treaty was concluded. Though main objective of the East India Company was to expand trade in this region centering round Nepal, the gateway of Tibet, and through it to West China. But gradually the East India Company got involved into internal administration and began to interfere in the internal affairs of the Cooch Behar State. Before the intervention of the British, Cooch Behar State had an independent-character from all respects. It is noted earlier that the East India Company did not annex the Cooch Behar though it is clearly mentioned in Third Article of the treaty that "The Raja will acknowledge subjection to the English East India Company upon his country being cleared off his enemies, and will allow the Cooch Behar country to be annexed to the Province of Bengal".[1]

During the twentieth century, European and non-European scholars have tried to give the definition of "Indirect Rule". According to them Indirect Rule stands to mean – (i) the continuity of the pre-colonial dynasty as 'native authority'. (ii) the pre-colonial territorial jurisdiction is maintained (iii) the native authority collects taxes and control budget; (iv) these native authorities continue to apply and enforce the traditional legal system (although it may be purged of abuses) (v) the native authorities appoint their subordinate officials; (vi) European Political Officers advise the native authorities and control matters which transcend the local jurisdiction of individual native authorities; and (viii) the native authorities serve as legislative bodies.[2] All these characteristics and practices could be found in the case of Cooch Behar State.

Before 1839, Cooch Behar State did not change because Harendra Narayan opposed the British policy. But after Harendra Narayan, the Cooch Behar State became the puppet in the hands of the British Government. After 1857, by the Queen's Proclamation, the British Government followed a general policy towards India. It has been seen the traditional and hereditary title of the Rulers of Cooch Behar was 'Maharaja", but in the year 1862 the granting of *Sunnad* conferring on the Raja of Cooch Behar turned into of "Maharaja Bahadur".[3] The British government introduced some reforms in the administration of the state, the feudal character of the administration gradually took a shape of a constitutional monarchy. On the other hand, the British Political Regent took a responsibility to guide the Maharaja of Cooch Behar not only in administration but also and other policymaking including education.

It has already been stated earlier that major Indian states and their rulers exercised varying degrees and types of sovereign powers before they entered into treaty relations with the British. But from the late eighteenth and early nineteenth centuries, the British as a matter of policy began to restrict the sovereignty of Indian rulers. These were the mechanisms, as they (British) followed were as such that by supplying military personnel, subsidies or tribute payments, purchase of commercial goods at favorable prices, and limited opportunities for other alliances. After 1857, the British developed a theory of indirect rule that helped to maintain hegemony in India without any further annexation and with the least possible expenditure of personnel and economic resources.[5]

The survival of Cooch Behar State was assured, but the State had to remain content with a feudatory status. Her independence was drastically curtailed; her autonomy was denied in practice, even though sometimes upheld in theory. Their right to mintage and of coining money were first restricted and gradually taken away.[6] Infact, the Paramount power retained the substance of administrative authority and economic policy in its own hands, leaving the shadow for the state. The British Political officers, designated either as Resident or Political Agent, were deputed to the state mainly to watch over the Proceedings of the *Durbars*. These officers were instructed to assist the ruling chiefs in solving their problems of the state, to promote British interests and also to counteract hostile forces.[7]

The British Government got an opportunity to introduce some reforms in the administration of the State. It has been shown how the Government assumed charge of the administration of Cooch Behar and placed it under the management of the British Commissioners. It is to be noted that the British Government banned minting coins in Raja's name and Government also maintained own Police forces in Cooch Behar. Not only that the references have been made as to the minority period of the Maharajas when the affairs of the State were being managed by the Regents. For example, as has been stated during the time of Maharaja Harendra Narayan (1801-1839AD)[8], the British government could not introduce judicial reforms in Cooch Behar State because of his unwillingness. But after Harendra Narayan, the Government established 'RajSabha', the highest Court of the Cooch Behar in 1840.[9] In the same time the State jurisdiction was divided into 'Civil' and 'Criminal' which were represented by Courts.[10] During the time of Maharaja Nripendra Narayan, the British Government established the 'State Council' in 1883, for interference of internal administration.[11] The state council formed with His Highness as President, other three members Superintendent of the State (Commissioner of British Government), a Dewan and a Judicial Officer. The Superintendent controlled indirectly all the departments and judicial department was under his direct control. During 1941, the State council was changed and new name was given as "Legislative Council" and formation of Legislative Council, which has been discussed in chapter VII.

Through our research we have seen that on the other objectives of the British Government was to collect money and to stabilize the economic condition of the Cooch Behar State.[12] Accordingly, the Commissioners took various reformative measures to develop the revenue administration. It may be noted that State economy was based on agriculture but nothing-definite system of land tenure, mode of assessment of revenue, total quantity of land or its distribution systems were known to the Maharajas of Cooch Behar. There were two types of lands – (a) Revenue paying land and (b) Rent free land. In 1774, Charles Purling, Collector of Rangpur, prepared Hust-o-Bud or Account of the annual land revenue of Cooch Behar.[13] In 1790, *Ijardari* system was introduced by Henry Douglas for land revenue collection in the state.

In 1870 and from 1872, as has been established that the land survey was concluded by orders of Sir George Campbell (Lieutenant Governor of Bengal), the *Ijardari* system was abolished and *Khas* collection was introduced in 1872.[14] The first land revenue settlement of Cooch Behar was concluded in 1877 by W.O.A. Backett (Assistant Commissioner). The re-settlement of 1886 was known as the *Rakam Charcha* Settlement and was extended in 1927.[15] Another settlement was given effect to from 1927-1928 were about to expire in 1956.[16] It is noteworthy that the whole settlement was prepared on the basis of the new survey under the supervision of British Commissioners of Cooch-Behar State. Revenue from other sources also supervised by the Commissioner. New methods and reforms were introduced by efficient British Commissioners for the development of land revenue of the state.

It is accepted that at first, the East India Company's Government was reluctant to assume the responsibility of educating the people of India. Although the Charter Act of 1813 was the first legislative admission of the claim of Indian education on the government's revenue, and allotted not less than a lakh of rupees every year for the "revival and improvement of literature", and "the introduction and Promotion of a knowledge of the sciences".[17] In 1853, the British Parliament for the first time "investigated seriously and sympathetically the development of Indian education.[18] Then gradually, the western education was spread all over the India and so a systematic educational policy was taken by the British Government. The Hunter Commission (1882) laid a special emphasis on the promotion of elementary mass education in the traditional method.

During nineteenth century, one can fined that the progress in respect of education was very slow in the state of Cooch Behar. However we have seen how at the time of Maharaja Narendra Narayan, a Vernacular school was started in the town of Cooch Behar in 1857 for the education of the children from the Royal blood. The British government was reluctant to spread education, which may be taken as for the masses and general people of the state. But the Government had a policy to educate the Princes of the State and they percolated the alien culture to the Royal family from the beginning of its interaction in different forms. For example as we have seen in the case of Colonel Jenkins who came to Cooch Behar as a Commissioner, and his first task was to introduce the English education in the state in 1861. After that, in 1870, R. Robinson was appointed as the first Superintendent of education in the State. Gradually, steps were taken to introduce the Primary, Secondary and Higher education and there was radical change in the education system, if not an education for the public. Incidentally during the time of Maharaja Nripendra Narayan, Cooch Behar got modernized and the most important factor was the spread of western education in Cooch Behar. Maharajas and people of Cooch Behar had however, not rejected western education and culture and it blossomed into its full form during Maharaja Narendra Narayan.

The interference of the British can also be found in the public health systems of the state. The initiatives of the Government to introduce a modern medical system have already been stated in chapter-IV.

Cooch Behar had also experienced a developed urban system and the concern for the same was reflected in the formation of a Town Committee to look after the town and town life of Cooch Behar as a whole. The growth of urban centers in different parts of Cooch Behar was related with the communication system and as has been stated that the kings as well as the British officials had given sufficient preference for the cause and it resulted in the economic development of the state during the time of our study.

If one is to look at the other side of the history of the state at the fag end of the 1940s when whole of India was passing through some political turmoil in respect of anti colonial movement, fact remains that the state of Cooch Behar was fully independent in between 1947-1949. The fate was however hanging on the question whether it would either join with India or Pakistan. Although it is not within the purview of our study it is suffix to conclude that the last Maharaja Jagaddipendra Narayan (reign period 1922-1949) was interested to join with India.Accordingly on 28th of August, 1949, the Cooch Behar was to accede to India when it finally signed the "Cooch Behar Merger Agreement". After two weeks on 12th September, 1949, Cooch Behar was again incorporated in the Indian Union as a Chief Commissioner's province. In the last phase by the States' Merger (West Bengal) Order 1949, issued on 31st December, 1949 under section 290A of the Govt. of India Act. 1935, Cooch Behar was transferred to and merged with the province of West Bengal on 1st January, 1950.

NOTES AND REFERENCES

1. S.C. Ghosal, *A History of Cooch Behar,* 1942, p. 408.
2. Michael H. Fisher, *Indirect Rule in India: Residents and the Residency system 1764-1858,* Delhi, 1991, p. 5.
3. *Cooch Behar Select Records,* Vol. II, 1888, p. 256.
4. Barbara N. Ramusack, *The Indian Princes and their States,* 2004, p. 130.
5. Ajit Kr. Neogy, *The Paramount Power and the Princely States of India,* p. 301.
6. *Ibid,* p. 302.
7. Ratna Roy Sanyal, *A Study of Anglo-Cooch Behar Relations 1772-1839,* p. 168.
8. H.N.Chaudhury, *The Cooch Behar State and its Land Revenue Settlement,* p. 304.
9. *Ibid.,* p. 306.
10. Durga Das Majumdar, *West Bengal District Gazetteer, Koch Behar,* 1977, p. 106.
11. *Annual Adminsitrative Report of Cooch Behar State,* 1882-1883, p. 6.
12. *Cooch Behar Select Records,* Vol. I, p. 234.
13. *Durga Das Majumdar, op.cit.,* p. 150.
14. Bhagabati Ch. Bandhopadhaya, *A History of Cooch Behar (Bengali),* p. 142.
15. S.C. Ghosal, *op. cit.* p.205.
16. *Annual Administrative Report of Cooch Behar State,* 1927-1928, p.12.
17. *East India Company's Act of 1813,* Section 43, p. 22.
18. N.R. Roy (ed.), *Western Colonial Policy,* Vol. II, p. 58.

Appendix-I

Chronology of Cooch Behar dynasty from 1773-1947

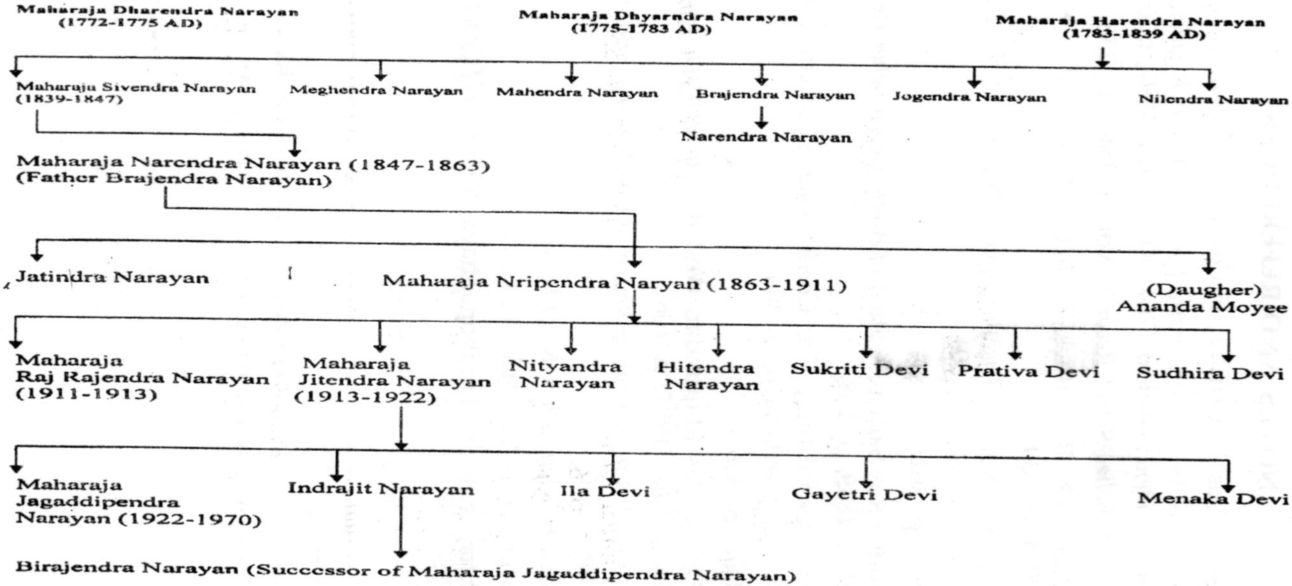

Source: Hemanta Kumar Roy Barma, (ed) Ranjit Dev, *Cooch Beharer Itihasa*, 2005.

APPENDIX -II

SUBJECTS ON WHICH THE COMMISSIONERS MERCER AND CHAUVET WERE ORDERED TO ENQUIRE AND REPORT.

Article – 1

That they enquire into the nature of the Behar Government previous to its being connected with the company in 1773, distinguishing between the real and nominal powers of the Rajahs, the Nazir and the Dewan Deo.

Article – 2

That they ascertain by what laws the succession to the Raj is regulated and whether the offices of Nazir Deo and Dewan Deo, are hereditary or in the immediate gift of the Rajah.

Article – 3

That they enquire whether the Tripartite Division of the Revenues between the Rajah, the Nazir Deo and the Dewan Deo, was real or nominal, and whether the two had the power of collecting and appropriating the proportions allotted to them without the control of the Rajah.

Article – 4

That upon the accession of a rajah, what are the ceremonies which the Dewan Deo and Nazir Deo, are entitled to perform in virtue of their offices, and how far they are considered as requisite to the regular investiture of the Rajah.

Article – 5

That they report upon the nature of the treaty concluded between the company and the Behar family in 1772, and whether the amount of the tribute is equal to the proportion stipulated.

Article – 6 & 7

That they ascertain whether the company's tribute was in arrears at the death of the late Raja Derjinder Narain to the Ranny, appointing her guardian to the infant Rajah, and inventing her with the management of the country during his minority.

That they enquire (whether any and what court exist in Cooch Behar) how far the Ranny had the management of affairs during the life of the late Raja and whether Sarbananda was the minister of his own choice or not.

Article – 8

That they ascertain whether the company's tribute was in Arrears at the death of the late Rajah Derjinder Narain, and whether there were any grounds for apprehending that it would not have been regularly paid if the Ranny had been continued in the management, and whether the appointment o the Nazir, Deo, did not tend to increase the divisions among the family by enabling him to prosecute his own views in prejudice to the rights of the Rajah and Ranny.

Article -9

That they enquire whether any and what courts exist in Cooch Behar for the administration of Civil and Criminal justice, and to whom the charge of these jurisdictions is committed, and point out to the Board such alterations in their constitution as they may deem best calculated to protect the lives and poverty of the inhabitants.

Article – 10

That they enquire by what mode the tribute has been collected from the district since the year 1772 whether it has been paid by the Rajah's Agents into the Treasury at Rungpore or whether collected from the country by a Suzawul or other person deputed by the collector. Whether the Tribute has ever been increased or diminished, and the causes of any variation that may have taken place.

Article – 11

That they ascertain the relation in which the Chacklas of Bodah, Patgong and Poorbbhag stand to the Behar family and the Company, and what are the nature of the Nazir Deo's claims upon the same alluded in his petitions to the Board.

Article -12

That they enquire who are the most proper persons to be entrusted with the guardianship of the Rajah and the management of the country during his minority.

Article – 13

That as the Behar family has sometimes been represented as labouring under extreme poverty and at others enjoying a considerable degree of Opulence they particularly enquire into the state of that family, their property and connections, and endeavor to ascertain the amount of the Money and effects carried off from the Raja's house by the party under Dhangar Deo, in order that the same may be resorted to the, or the amount levied on the properly of the insurgents should it be deemed expedient to cause such retribution to be made.

Article -14

That they enquire into such Unions as the Deb Rajah

may have made on the Behar family either for money or effects or for supposed encroachments upon his Territories provided the same have not been already adjusted.

Article – 15

That they adjust the Rajahs Accounts with the Nazir Deo and Sham Chander, should they be yet unsettled, and enquire into any claims the Rajah may have on Ramkisson. That they likewise ascertain whether any of the Behar family have taken upon sums of money on loan from the Company's Civil or Military Servants, and whether such loans have been settled or are unadjusted.

Article – 16 & 17

That they ascertain whether the charges made by the Ranny and the Nazir Deo, against each other had any foundation, and whether the Rajah and Ranny were influenced by Surbanand to make those complaints or by their aversion to Nazir Deo's being enrusted with the management of the district: that they enquire whether the letters written by them, from Berhampur declaring that the family disputes had been amicably settled, and that they were desirous of committing the management of the country to the son of the Nazir Deo, were written by their own consent. Or in consequence of any compulsion exercised by the adherents of the Nazir Deo.

Article -18 & 19

That they enquired into the nature of the Military Establishment kept up by the Rajah under the Command of Leutenant Duncanson, the mode in which it was paid and the services in which it was employed.

Article -20

That they report upon the state of the Mint and the coinage in the District of Cooch Behar.

Article – 21

That they enquire in to the state of the commerce and manufactures of the country.

Article – 22

That copies of all the proceedings respecting the disturbances in Cooch Behar since the death of the Late Rajah Derjinder Narain, by transmitted to them by the Secretary together with a copy of the Treaty entered in the between the Company and the Bhootaneers in 1744, and an order issue to the collector of Rangpur to Furnish the with whatever Records they may require from his office, and to afford them every assistance and information in his power to enable them to effect the objects of their deputation.

APPENDIX—III

AGREEMENT OF MERGER OF THE COOCH BEHAR STATE

A Collateral Letter of V.P. Menon, Advisor to the Government of India, Ministry of States, to Jagaddipendra Narayan Bhup Bahadur, Maharaja of Cooch Behar, about the merger of Cooch Behar State.

D.O. No. 15 (19)-F/49

Ministry of States

New Delhi

The 30th August, 1949

MY DEAR MAHARAJ SAHIB

In connection with the Agreement concluded between the Governor General of India and Your Highness for the integration of Cooch Behar State Your Highness raised certain points for clarification, the Government of India has considered them and accepts the following arrangements:

(1) It is the intention of the Government of India to administer for the present territories of Cooch Behar State as a centrally administered area under a Chief Commissioner.

(2) All contracts and agreement entered into by Your Highness before date on which the administration is made over to the Government of India will be honoured except in so far as any of these contracts or agreements is either repugnant to the provision of any law made applicable to the State or inconsistent with the general policy of the Government.

(3) The Allowances at present drawn by her Highness the Rajmata will be continued for her lifetime and will be

paid out of the revenues of the State. Your Highness' brother and other members of the Ruling Family will also be paid allowances from the revenues of the State as per list attached.

(4) The responsibility for the Cooch Behar State Forces will be taken over by the Government of India from 12th September 1949. If these forces are disbanded or any of the men discharged they will receive the pension or gratuity or compensation to which they may be entitled under the rules of the State.

(5) Adequate grants will be provided to for the protection of Your Highness' person and palace.

(6) No land or building being Your Highness' private property shall be requisitioned or acquired without payment of full compensation.

(7) Electricity from the State Power House for the main residence of Your Highness and family within the State will be provided at the fixed rate in existence immediately before the transfer of administration to Government of India. Water supply will be provided free of charge to the main palace of Your Highness and family within the State.

(8) The management of the temples and Debuttar properties in the State may be entrusted to a Trust which shall consist of Your Highness as President, 3 nominees of Your Highness and 2 nominees of Government. This Trust will be in charge of all temples both inside and outside the State. In the even of the abolition of the zamindars which are Debuttar property, Government will ensure that the Trust has adequate resources to fulfill its object.

(9) Your Highness may create a Trust for the marriage of the son and daughter of Isharani of Cooch Behar with a corpus of Rs. 1 lakh. The trustees will be besides Your Highness, Their Highness of Jaipur and Dewas Junior.

(10) The Civil List of Reserve Fund of Rs. 10,60,900 shall be Your Highness' private property and shall be held by Your Highness in Trust for meeting expenditure in connection with Your Highness' private property and shall be held by Your Highness in Trust for meeting expenditure

in connection with Your Highness' marriage or specials repairs to the palace and any unforeseen expenditure.

(11) The administration of the Maharajkumar Fund with a corpus of Rs. 486900 shall be formally vested in a Trust which Your Highness and Their Highness of Jaipur and Dewas Junior shall be trustees.

(12) Your Highness will be entitled to hold customary Durbar and troops present at the capital will take part in the Dasserah and other celebrations.

(13) Your Highness will retain your present rank in the Indian Army.

(14) Government will endeavour to associate the name Narayan with the Cooch Behar State Forces even after their absorption in the Indian Army.

The Ministry of States has issued a Memorandum on the privileges and dignities which has been finalized in consultation with the Rajpramukhs of Unions and other States. Your Highness will see that the Memorandum deals adequately with the various suggestions made by the Rulers from time to time regarding their rights and privileges.

With kind regards

Yours sincerely

V.P. Menon

COOCH BEHAR MERGER AGREEMENT

Agreement made this Twenty-eight day of August 1949 between the Governor-General of India and His Highness the Maharaja of Cooch Behar.Where as in the best interests of the State of Cooch Behar as well as of the Dominion of India it is desirable to provide for the administration of the said State by or under the authority of the Dominion Government.

It is hereby agreed as follows -

Article I

His Highness the Maharaja of Cooch Behar hereby cedes to the Dominion Government full and exclusive authority, jurisdiction and powers for and in relation to .the governance of the State and agrees to transfer the administration of the State to the Dominion Government on the 12th day of September 1949 (hereinafter referred to as "the said day").As from the said day the Dominion Government will be competent to exercise the said powers, authority and jurisdiction in such manner anon through such agency as it may think fit.

Article 2

His Highness the Maharaja shall continue to enjoy the same personal rights, privileges, dignities and titles which he would have enjoyed had this agreement not been made.

Article 3

His Highness the Maharaja shall with effect from the said day be entitled to receive for his life-time from the revenues of the State annually for his privy purse the sum of Rupees eight lakhs fifty thousand free of all taxes. After him the privy purse will be fixed at Rupees seven lakhs only. This amount is intended to cover all the expenses of the Ruler and his family, including expenses on account of his personal staff, maintenance of his residences, marriages and other ceremonies, etc., and will neither be, increase candor reduced for any reason whatsoever.

The Government of India undertakes that the said sum of Rupees eight lakhs fifty thousand shall be paid to His Highness the Maharaja in four equal, installments in advance at the beginning of each quarter from the State Treasury or at such Treasury as may be specified by the Government of India.

Article 4

His Highness the Maharaja shall be entitled to the full ownership, use and enjoyment of all private properites (as distinct from State properties) belonging to him on the date of this agreement.

His Highness the Maharaja will furnish to the Dominion Government before the l5th September, 1949, an inventory of all the immovable property, securities and cash balances held by him as such private property.

If any dispute arises as to whether any item of property is the private property of His Highness the Maharaja or State property, it shall be referred to a Judicial officer qualified to he appointed as High Court Judge, and the decision of that officer shall be final and binding on both parties.

Article 5

All the members of his Highness' family shall be entitled to all the personal privileges, dignities and titles' enjoyed by them whether within or outside the territories of the State, immediately before the 15th day of August t947.

Article 6

The Dominion Government guarantees the succession according to law rend custom, to the giddy of the State and to tiles Highness the Maharaja's personal rights, privileges, dignities and titles.

Article 7

No enquiry shall be made by or under the authority of the Movement of India, and no proceedings shall lie in any Court in Cooch Behar' against His

Highness the Maharaja, whether in a personal capacity or otherwise, in respect of anything done or orbited to be done by him or under his authority during the period of his administration of that State.

Article 8

(l) The Government of India hereby guarantees either the continuance in service of the permanent members of the Public Services of Cooch Behar on conditions which will be not less advantageous than those on which they were serving before the date on which the administration .of Cooch Behar is made over to the Government of India or the payment of reasonable

(2) The Government of India further guarantees the continuance of pensions and leave salaries sanctioned by His Highness the Maharaja to servants of the State who have retired or proceeded on leave preparatory to retirement, before the date on which the administration of Cooch Behar is made over to the Government of India.

Article 9

Except with the previous sanction of the Government of India no proceedings. civil and criminal, shall be instituted against any person in Aspect of any act done or purporting to be done in the excretion of his duties as a servant of the State before the day on which the administration is made over to the Government of India.

In confirmation whereof Mr. Vapal Pangunni Menon, Advisor to the Government of India in the Ministry of States has appended his signature on behalf and with the authority of the Governor General of India and Lieutenant Colonel His Highness the Maharaja Jagaddipendranarayan Bhup Bahadur, Maharaja of Cooch Behar, has appended his signature on behalf of himself, his heirs and successors.

JAGADDIPENDRANARAYN
Maharaja of Cooch Behar

V.P.MENON
Advisor to the Govt. of India
Ministry of States

APPENDIX—IV

Letter No. 40

[The exact copy of the original letter written by Jenkins, Agent to the governor-general, North East Frontier to Maharaja Narendra Narayan, Cooch Behar on January 7, 1861.]

Gowhatty 7 Jany /61

My dear Rajah,

I have had the pleasure of receiving your letter of the 28th Ulto. for which I beg to return you my thanks. —

I am very glad to learn you are commencing on Pucka Buildings for the different offices round the Large Tank, a Record Room is required of the first necessity, and I hope it will be completed early. — The other works are almost equally requisite and I shall watch their progress with much interest. — I am obliged to you for laying the foundation of the

on my name, and I hope you
will take measures to provide
[illegible] being a prosperous Institution
— The first thing is to have proper
well educated Masters and to
place it under efficient Super-
intendence — I have seen that
you propose placing it under
[illegible] superintendence,
and I think you would do well to select
[illegible] man — [illegible] liberal
[illegible] self and appears to me to
take sincere pleasure in promoting
education — But who are
your Masters and with defined
authority! — I look to great benefit
to your people from this
School — it is impossible that
any one will now be content
with the old state of things

and you must conform
to the new as well as the
rest of the world and for
the advancement of your
kingdom to enable it to keep
pace with the surrounding dis-
-tricts an improvement in the
education of the mass of the
people is the one thing essential.
I think well of your
proposal to get up Kishory
Chand Mitter — notwithstanding
his being ejected in Calcutta, there
is no doubt but he is a well
educated gentleman and an
able efficient officer. How
are you to provide for the pre-
-sent [illegible] If you can however
do so & remove him without
giving much offence I am satis-
-fied you will be doing what
is very desirable — you will
not only possess a competent
Dewan but you will have a
friend whose interests in
Calcutta may be serviceable

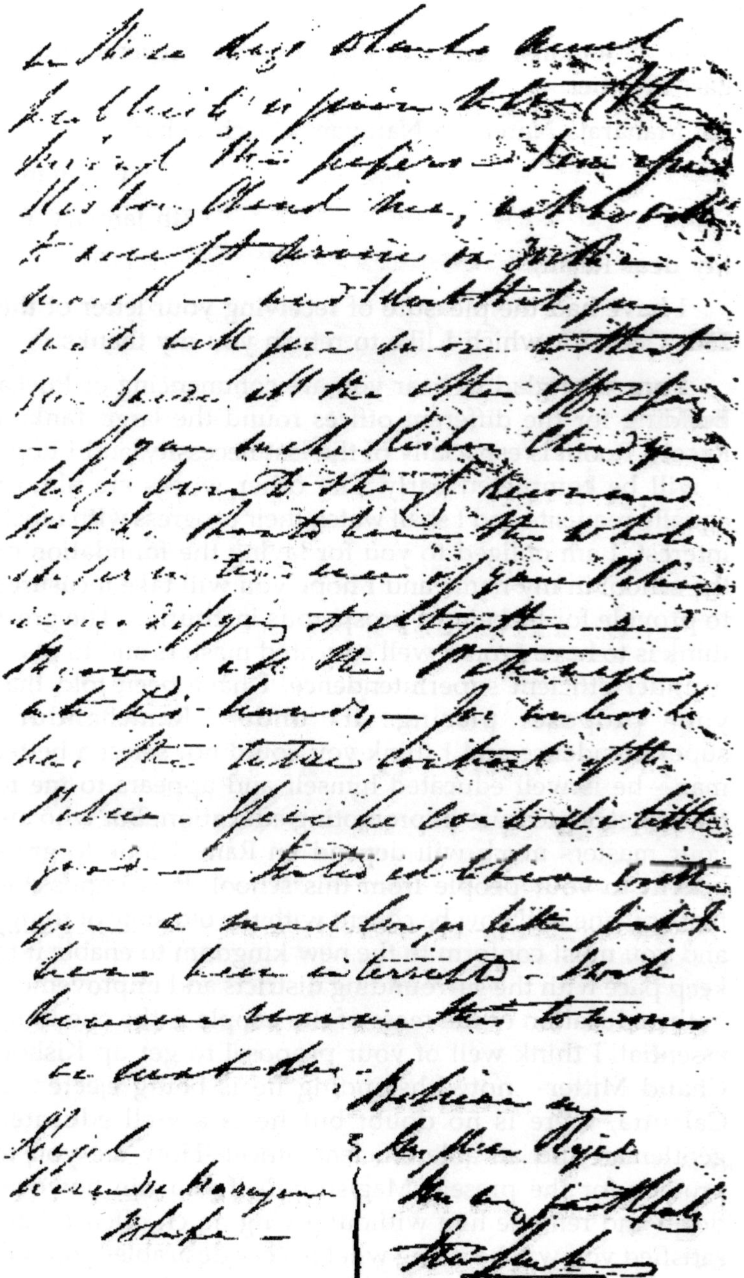

Letter No. 40

From: F. Jenkins, Agent to the Governor General, North East Frontier

To: Maharaja Narendra Narayan, Cooch Behar

Gawhatty,

7th January, 61.

My dear Rajah,

I have had the pleasure of receiving your letter of the 28th Octo. for which I like to return you my thanks.

I am very glad to hear you are commencing of Pucka Building for the different offices round the large Tank, a Record Room is especially of the last necessity, and I hope it will be completed early. The other works are almost equally requisite and I shall watch their progress with much interest. I am obliged to you for laying the foundation of the school in my name and I hope you will take measures to provide for its being a prosperous institution. The great think is to have proper well educated masters and to place it under efficient superintendence. I have been told that you propose placing it under Ramchandur's superintendence and I think you could not select a better man-- he is well educated himself and appears to me to take sincere pleasure in promoting education. But who are your masters much will depend on Ram. I look to great benefit to your people from this school. It is impossible that any one will now be conent with the old state of things and you must conform to the new kingdom to enable it to keep pace with the surrounding districts and improvement in the education of the mass of the people is the one thing essential. I think well of your proposal to get up Kishori Chand Mitter-- notwithstanding he is being ejected in Calcutta, there is no doubt but he is a well educated gentleman and an able efficient officer--How are you to provide for the present Magistrate?--if you can however do so and remove him without giving much offence I am satisfied you will be doing what is very desirable--you will not only possess a competent Magistrate--but you will gain a friend whose interests in Calcutta may be serviceable in these days when so much publicity is given to these things through the papers-- I am afraid Kishori Chand may not be willing to accept service on 300/- rupees a month--and I do not think you should well give more without you raise all the other office pay-- If you make Kishori Chand your Magistrate I would strongly recommend that he should have the whole superintendence of your police remodifying it altogether and this way all the Patronage into his hands- - for unless he has the entire control of the Police--I fear he could do little good--I intended to have written you amuch longer letter but I have been interrupted-- I will however resume this tomorrow or next day.

Believe me my dear Rajah

Your very faithfully,

Sd/F. Jenkins

Rajah Narendra Narayan Bhup

APPENDIX—V

NOTICE OF EXPULSION OF PANCHANAN BARMA FROM COOCH BEHAR STATE

Extract of Notification regarding Rai Saheb Panchanan Barman, a Jotedar of Cooch Behar.

And whereas the Council consider it necessary in the interest of the State, that the Rai Saheb Panchanan Barman should be prevented from carrying on a mischevous propaganda in the State and also to mark their displeasure at his disloyal and scandalous conduct in getting up the forged petition referred to above and utilizing in a manner calclulated to bring Her Highness the Maharani Regent and the Regency Administration generally into contempt with the subject of the State and the public generally and to create discontent in the State against Her Highness the Maharani Regent and the Regency Administration generally.

It is hereby ordered that the said Rai Saheb Panchanan Barman is prohibited from entering the State for a period of five years from the date this order is communicated to him without the special permission, previously obtained of Regency Council.

It is further ordered that, if at any time the said Rai Saheb Panchanan Barman enters into any part of the State in disobedience of this order, he will be liable to be arrested by the police and removed from the State and that he shall also be liable to prosecution and conviction, to be punished with simple imprisonment for a term which may extend to three months or with fine which may extent to five hundred rupees or both provided that no such prosecution will be undertaken except with the sanction of the Regency Council.

By Order

Sitesh Chandra Sanyal

Registrar, Regency Council

Cooch Behar

Cooch Behar Gazette, Part I

Page 120

APPENDIX—VI

Articles of a treaty between the Honourable East India Company and the Deva Raja or Raja of Bhutan.

1. That the Honourable Company, wholly from the consideration for district to which the Bhutias represent themselves to be reduced, and from the desire of living in peace with their neighbours, will relinquish the lands which belonged to Deva Raja before the commencement of the war with the Raja of Cooch Behar, namely, to the eastward of the lands of Chichakhata and Paglaghat, and to the westward of the lands of Kyranti, Maraghat and Luckeepore.

2. That, for the possession of the Chichakhata province, the Deva Raja shally pay an annual tribute of five Tangan horses to the Honouralble Company, which was the acknowledgement paid to the Cooch Behar Raja.

3. That, the Deva Raja shall deliver up Dhairjendra Narayan, Raja of Cooch Behar, together with his brother, the Dewan Deo, who is confined with him.

4. That the Bhutias, being merchants, shall have the same privileges of trade as formerly, without the payment of duties, and their caravan shall be allowed to go to Rangpore annually.

5. That, the Deva Raja shall never cause incursions to be made into the country, nor in any respect whatever, molest the ryots, that have come under the Honourable Company's subjection.

6. That, if any ryot or inhabitant whatever, shall desert from the Honourable Company's territories, the Deb Raja shall cause them to be delivered up immediately upon application being made to him.

7. That, in case the Bhutias, or any one under the government of Deva Raja, shall have any demands upon, or disputes with any of the inhabitants of these or any part of the company's territories, they shall prosecute them by an application to the Magistrate who shall reside here for the administration of justice.

8. That, whatever Sannyasis are considered by the English as an enemy, the Deva Raja will not allow to take shelter in any part of the districts now given up, nor permit them to enter into the Honourable company's territories, or through any part of his; and if the Bhutias shall not of themselves be able to drive them out, they shall give information to the Resident on the part of the English

in Cooch Behar and they shall not consider the English troops pursuing the Sannyasis into these districts as any breach of this treaty.

9. That, in case the Honourable company shall have occasion for cutting timbers from any part of the woods under the Hills, they shall do it duty free, and people they send shall be protected.

10. That, there shall be a mutual release of prisoners.

This treaty to be signed by the Honourable President, and Council of Bengal, and the Honourable company's seal to be affixed on the one part, and to be signed and sealed by the Deva Raja on the other part.

Signed and ratified at the Fort William, the 25th of April, 1774.

(Signed) Warren Hastings,

William Andersey,

P.M. Daires,

Henry Goodwin,

H. Graham

George Vansitart

(A true copy)

(Signed) J. Auriol,

Assistant Secretary

APPENDIX—VII

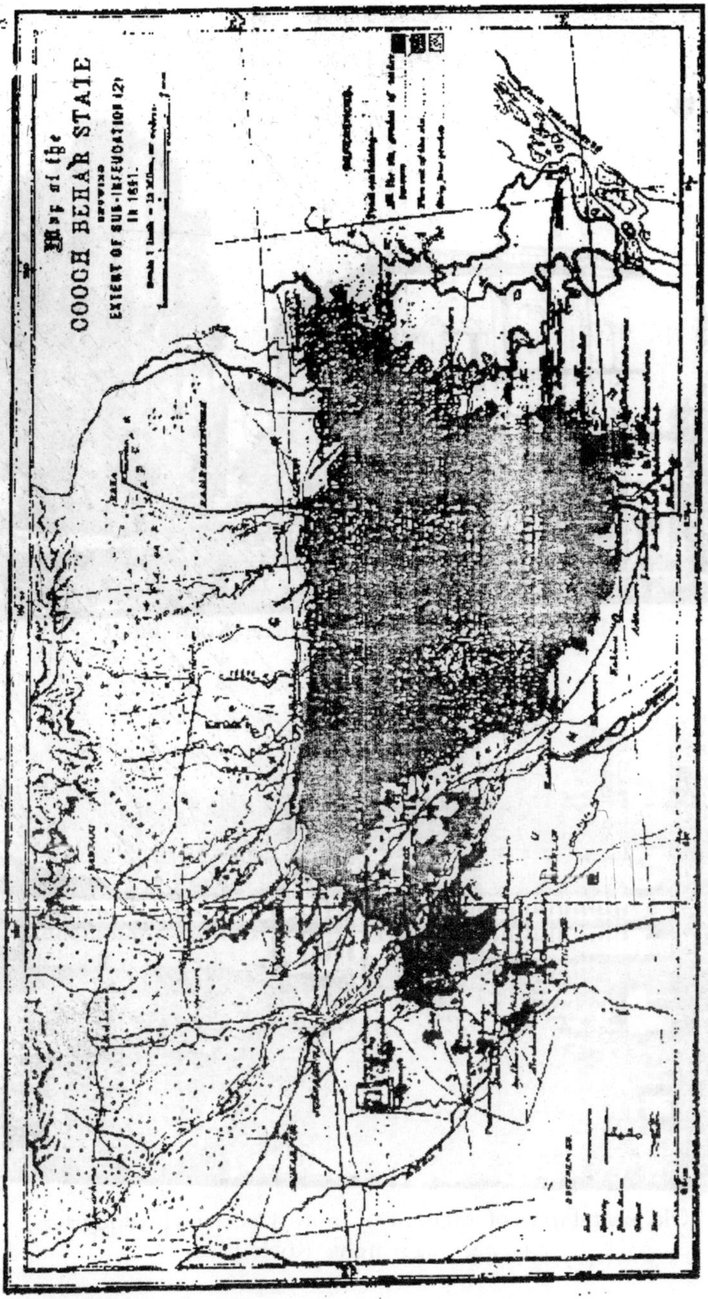

APPENDIX—VIII

Deputy Commissioner's officer, Koch Bihar

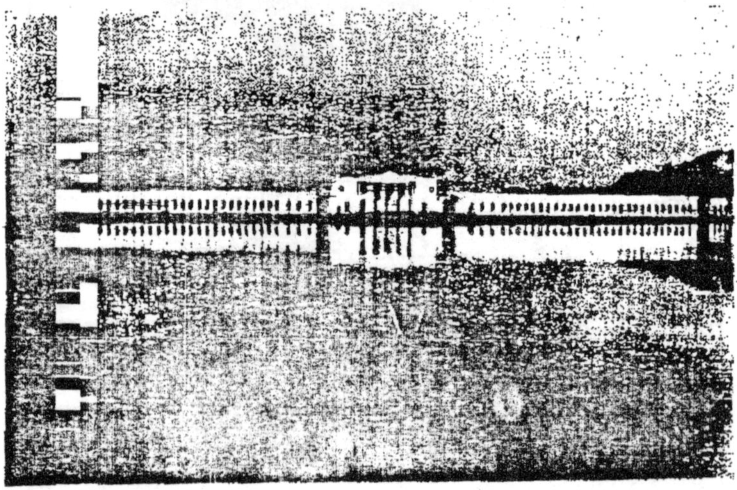

Old secretariat of Maharajas (now District Headquarters) facing Sagardighi, Koch Bihar

APPENDIX—IX

Place of Coronation of Princes

APPENDIX—X

Cooch Behar Palace

Gate way of Cooch Behar Palace

APPENDIX—XI

(1st Cooch Behar Infantry, Established in 16th Century and abolished in 1950)

(British Guard Battalions, Establishes in 1944)

Bibliography

1. Primary Sources

A. Letters and Proceedings

Board of Revenue Proceedings.

Cooch Behar State Govt. Important Correspondence of the Chaklajat, Calcutta, 1899.

Home Consultations.

Home Public Proceedings.

Letters to and from the Court of Directors.

Proceeding of the Governor General-in-Council.

Proceedings of the Government of Bengal, Judicial (Political) 1872.

The Proceedings of the Cooch Behar Hitaishini Sabha, 1272 B.S. Cooch Behar.

B. Reports

Annual Administrative Report of the Cooch Behar State.

Annual Education Report of the Cooch Behar State, 1910-11.

Beckett W.O.A., *Completion Settlement Report*, Cooch Bhear, 1874.

Cooch Behar Census Report, 1951.

Firminger. W.K., *Fifth Report of the Select Committee,* Vol-I, Cal. 1917.

Jenkins, F. A., Report on Koch Behar, 1849 in Selections from the Records of the

Government of Bengal, No-5, Calcutta, 1851.

Glazier. G.E. *A Report on the District of Rang pore,* Calcutta, 1873.

Mercer and Chauvet's *Report on Cooch Behar in 1788,* Cooch Behar, 1869.

Milligan, J. A., Final Reports on the Survey and Settlement ør the Jalpaiguri, Cal, 1919.

Pemberton, R.B., *Report on Bootan,* Calcutta, 1865.

Report of Richard Temple, *Boards of Revenue Proceedings,* 1875.

Sanders, I., *Settlement Report on Western Dooars,* Calcutta, 1895.

C. Journals and Gazetteers :

Ananda Bazar Patrika, January 1st, 1950.

Cooch Bhear Darpan, 9th year, 10th Edition, 1383 B.S.

Griffth. W. *Journal of travels in Assam,* Burma, Bootan etc, Cal, 1847.

Hooker, J. D., *Himalayan Journal of Travels in Assam,* Burma, Bootan, etc, Calcutta, 1847.

Imperial Gazetteer of India (Eastern Bengal and Assam), Cal, 1909.

Imperial Gazetteer of India, Vol-2, London, 1885.

Journal of James Rennel, Vol-3, 1910.

Journal of the Asiatic Society of Bengal, 1788-1953, 1956.

Madhuparni, Coch Behar District Special Issues, 1990.

Sahitya Sabha Patrika, Cooch Behar, 1380 B.S.

The East India Gazetteer, Walter Hamilton.

West Bengal District Gazetteers, Koch Behar, Durgadas Majumdar, 1977.

D. Records and Books

Aitchison C. U., *Collection of Treaties, Engagements and Sanads Relating to India,* Vol-I-II, Calcutta, 1909.

Cooch Behar State Government, *Cooch Behar Select Records* Vol-I, 1882;

Vol-2, Cooch Behar, 1884.

Forrest, G.W., *Selections from the letters, Dispatches and other State Papers,*

Preserved in the Foreign Department, Govt. of India, Vol-III, Cal, 1890.

Gleig, G.R, *Memoirs of Warren Hastings,* Vol-3, London, 1841.

Hunter, W.W., *Statistical Account of Bengal,* Vo-X, London, 1879.

Martin, M., *Wellesley Correspondence,* London, 1964.

Nicolas Rhodes and Sankar K. Bose, *The Coinage of Cooch Behar,* Dhubri, 1999.

Ralph Fitch, *Early Travels in India,* (ed) W. Foster, London, 1921.

Ross, *Cornwallis Correspondence,* London, 1964.

Sen, S.N., *Prachin Bangla Patra Sankalan* (Bengal Version), Cal, 1942.

V. Sankar (ed), *Sardar Patel: Select Correspondernces,* 1945-1950, Vol-2 Delhi.

2. Secondary Sources

A. **Bengali**

Bandyopadhyaya, Bhagabati Charan, *Koch Beharer Itihas,* Cooch Behar, 1882.

Barma, Dharma Narayan, *Maharaja Nara Narayan,* Calcutta, 1978.

De, Krishnendu (ed), *Cooch Behar Parikroma,* Cooch Behar, 1984.

Ghosh, Ananda Chandra, *Cooch Beharer Itihas,* (ed) by Ananda Gopal ghosh and Narayan Chandra Saha, Darjeeling, 1990.

Chakraborty, Jadav Chandra, *Cooch Beharer Sankhipta Itihas,* Cooch Behar, 1983.

Khan Chaudhruy, Amanatullah Ahmed, *Cooch Beharer Itihas*, Vol-I, Cooch Behar, 1936.

Pal, Nripendra Nath (ed), *Bisay Cooch Behar*, Calcutta, 1994.

Roy, Hemanta Kumar, Barma, *Cooch Beharer Itihas*, Cooch Behar, 1981.

B. English

Acharyya N.N., *Assam and Neighbouring States*, New Delhi, 1983.

Acharyya N.N., *North East - as Viewed by Foreigners*, Gauhati, 1985.

Ashton, S.R., *British Policy towards the Indian States 1905-1939*, London, 1982.

Auber, P., *Rise and progress of British Power in India*, Vol-I, London, 1873.

Banerjee, A.C., *The Eastern Frontier of British India*, Calcutta, 1934.

Banerjee, Anil Chandra., *The Rajput States and British Paramountcy*, New Delhi, 1980.

Banerjee, D. N., *Early Administrative System of the East India Company in Bengal*, London, 1943.

Bhattacharjee, S. N., *A History of Mughal North East Frontier Policy*, Calcutta, 1929.

Barbara, N. Ramusack. *The Indian Princess and their States*, Cambridge University Press, 2004.

Bingle, R.J, *Changing Attitudes to the Indian States, 1820-1850: A study of Oudh, Hyderabad and*

and Jaipur, New Delhi, 1972.

Buckland, C.E., *Bengal under the Lieutenant Governors from 1854 to 1898*, Vols-I-II, Delhi, 1976.

Bhuyan, S. K., *Anglo-Assamese Relations (1771-1826)*, Gauhati, 1949.

Campbell, *Glimpses of Bengal*, Calcutta, 1907.

Chakraborty, A.K., *Literature in Kamata Koch Behar Raj Darbar*, Calcutta, 1988.

Chatterjee, Suniti Kumar., *Kirata Jana Kriti*, Reprint, Calcutta, 1998.

Chaudhuri, Dipak Kumar., *The Political Agents and the Native Raj*, New Delhi, 1999.

Chaudhuri, K.N, Dewey, C.J.(ed), *Economy and Society*, Delhi, 1979.

Chaudhury, S.B., *Civil Disturbance during the British Rule in India (1765-1867)*, Calcutta, 1955.

Chaudhury, H.N., *The Cooch Behar State and its Land Revenue Settlement*, Cooch Behar, 1903.

Chudgar, P.L.,*Indian Princes under British Protection*, New Delhi, 1986.

Copland,I.,*The British Raj and the Indian Princes: Paramountcy in western*

India 1857-1930, New Delhi, 1982.

Creagh Cooen, Terence, *The Indian Political Service: A Study in Indirect Rule*, London, 1971.

Curtis, Lionel., *Dyarchy 1919*, Oxford, 1920.

Das, Biswanath (ed), *Memoirs of Maharani Suniti Devi of Cooch Behar*, New Delhi, 1995.

Das, Biswanath and Subhendu Majumdar, *Princely Cooch Behar, A Documentary study on Letters (1792-863)*, Calcutta, 1990.

Datta, J.C., *A Introduction to the History of Tripura from Monarchy to Democracy*, Calcutta, 1984.

Deb, Arabinda., *India and Bhutan*, Calcutta, 1976.

Devi, Gayatri, *A Princess Remembers*, New Delhi, 1995.

Dutta, S. C., *The North East and the Mughals*, Delhi, 1984.

Fisher, H. Michael, (ed), *The Politics of the British Annexation of India-1757- 1857*,

London, 1996.

Fisher, H.M., *Indirect Rule in India Resident and the Residency system 1764-1858*, London, 1988.

Fitze, K.S., *Twilight of the Maharaja*, London, 1956.

Gait, E.A., *A History of Assam*, Cal, 1906.

Ghosal, S.C., *History of Cooch Behar* (Trans), Cooch Behar, 1942.

Gopal, S., *British Policy in India 1858-1905*, Cambridge, 1965.

Hamilton, F., *Account of Assam* (ed), S.K. Bhuyan, Gouhati, 1940.

Hettne, Bjorne., *The Political Economy of Indirect Rule: Mysore 1881-1947*, London, 1978.

Jeffrrey, Robin (ed), *People, Princes and Paramount Power- Society and Politics in Indian Princely States*, New Delhi, 1978

Lee,Warner., *The Native States of India*, London, 1910.

Lee,Warner.,*The protected Princes of India*, London, 1894.

Low, D.A., *Lion Rampant: Essays in the study of British Imperialism*, London, 1973.

Martin, M., *The History, Atiquities etc. of Eastern India*, Vol-III, London, 1838.

Maharani, Gayatri Devi, *A Princess Remembers*, Calcutta, 1996.

Mehta, M.S., *Lord Hastings and the Indian States*, Bombay, 1930.

Menon, V.P., *The Story of the Integration of the Indian States*, Bombay, 1956.

Metcalf, Thomas, *The Aftermath of Revolt: India, 1857-1870*, London, 1964.

Misra, B.B., *The Central Administration of the East India Company 1773 1834*, Oxford, 1959.

Misra, Banky Bihari., *The Bureaucracy in India: An Historical Analysis of*

Development up to 1947, Delhi, 1977.

Misra, R.P. (ed), *Million Cities of India*, Delhi, 1977.

Neogi, A.K.,*The Paramount Power and the Princely States of India 1858-1881*, Cal, 1979.

Panikkar, K.M., *The Evolution of British Policy towards Indian States-1774-1858*, Cal, 1929,An Introduction to the study of Relations of the Indian States with the Government of India, London, 1927.

Ray, Mihir Kumar., *Princely States and the Paramount Power,1858-*

1876 : A Study of the Nature of Political Reletion between the British Government and the Indian States, New Delhi,1981.

Roberts P. William, *Empire of the Soul,* New York, 1994.

Roy S.C., *Land Revenue Administration in India,* Calcutta, 1915.

Roy Surendra Nath., *A History of the Native States of India,* Calcutta, 1888.

Sen, Jahar, *Essays in Indo-Nepal Trade,* New Delhi, 1991.

Sever, Adrian, (ed), Documents *and Speeches on the Indian Princely States,* Vol-II, Delhi, 1985.

Sidney, Low., *The Indian States and Ruling Princes,* London, 1929.

Singh, K. Natwar, *The Magnificent Maharaja: The Life and Times of Maharaja Bhupinder Singh of Patiala (1891-1938).*

Sundaram, K.V., *Urban and Regional Planning in India,* Delhi, 1977.

Sutherland, John., *Sketches of the Relations Subsisting between the British Government in* India and the Different Native States, Calcutta, 1837.

Thompson, Edward., *The Making the Indian Princes,* London, 1978.

Walia, Urmila., *Changing British Attitudes Towards the Indian States, 1823-1835,* New Delhi, 1985.

Yapp, Malcolm.,*Strategies of British India: Britain, Iran, and Afghanistan, 1758-1850,* Oxford, 1980.

C. Unpublished Ph.D. Dissertations

1. Sen, partha Kumar, *Study of some aspects of the history of Kamata Kochbehar since 1772 to the date of Accesion of Shivendra Narayan,* North Bengal University.
2. Das, Kamalesh Chandra, *Modernisation of a Princely State Cooch Behar under maharaja Nripendra Narayan (1863-1911),* North Bengal University.
3. Sircar, Sekhar, *Land Settlement and Revenue Administration and Taxation under the Maharajas of Cooch Behar State (1773-1949),* North Bengal University.

■■■